Bridges Across
the South

Pergamon Titles of Related Interest

Haq Dialogue For A New Order
Haq/Streeten Development Choices for the 1980s
Meagher An International Redistribution of Wealth
Menon Bridges Across the South

UNITAR-CEESTEM Library on NIEO

Laszlo & Kurtzman Eastern Europe and the New International Economic Order
Laszlo & Kurtzman Europe and the New International Economic Order
Laszlo & Kurtzman Political and Institutional Issues of the New International Economic Order
Laszlo & Kurtzman The Structure of the World Economy and the New International Economic Order
Laszlo & Kurtzman The United States, Canada and the New International Economic ORder
Laszlo et al. The Implementation of the New International Economic Order
Laszlo et al. World Leadership and the New International Economic Order
Laszlo et al. The Objectives of the New International Economic Order
Laszlo et. al. The Obstacles to the New International Economic Order
Lozoya & Bhattacharya The Financial Issues of the New International Economic Order
Lozoya & Cuadra Africa, Middle East and the New International Economic Order
Lozoya & Bhattacharya Asia and the New International Economic Order
Lozoya & Green International Trade, Industrialization and the New International Economic Order
Lozoya & Estevez Latin America and the New International Economic Order
Lozoya & Birgin Social and Cultural Issues of the New International Economic Order
Lozoya et al. Alternative Views of the New International Economic Order
Miljan, Laszlo & Kurtzman Food and Agriculture in Global Perspective

Related Journals*

Habitat International
Socio-Economic Planning Sciences
World Development

*Free specimen copies available upon request.

PERGAMON
POLICY
STUDIES

ON THE NEW INTERNATIONAL
ECONOMIC ORDER

Bridges Across the South

Technical Cooperation Among Developing Countries

B.P. Menon

Pergamon Press

NEW YORK • OXFORD • TORONTO • SYDNEY • FRANKFURT • PARIS

Pergamon Press Offices:

U.S.A.   Pergamon Press Inc., Maxwell House, Fairview Park, Elmsford, New York 10523, U.S.A.

U.K.   Pergamon Press Ltd., Headington Hill Hall, Oxford OX3 OBW, England

CANADA   Pergamon of Canada, Ltd. Suite 104, 150 Consumers Road, Willowdale, Ontario M2J 1P9, Canada

AUSTRALIA   Pergamon Press (Aust.) Pty. Ltd., P.O. Box 544, Potts Point, NSW 2011, Australia

FRANCE   Pergamon Press SARL, 24 rue des Ecoles, 75240 Paris, Cedex 05, France

**FEDERAL REPUBLIC   Pergamon Press GmbH, Hammerweg 6, Postfach 1305,
OF GERMANY**   6242 Kronberg/Schönberg, Federal Republic of Germany

Library of Congress Cataloging in Publication Data

Menon, Bhashkar P
  Bridges across the south.

  (Pergamon policy studes)
  Bibliography: p.
  Includes index.
  1. Underdeveloped areas. 2. Technical assistance.
3. International cooperation. I. Title.
HC59.7.M44 1980   309.2'232'1724   79-19278
ISBN 0-08-024645-1
ISBN 0-08-024646-x pbk.

Printed in the United States of America

Contents

Preface

In September 1977 I was asked by Dr. Abdel Razzak Abdel Meguid, then Deputy Secretary-General of the U.N. Conference on Technical Cooperation among Developing Countries (TCDC) to write a book about the Conference. He did not want an "official" book, with all the constraints on language and opinion that implied, but one written frankly for a general audience. He wanted it to appear before the Conference met in August 1978 in Buenos Aires.

As it turned out, this was not possible. I was, by some mysterious process, chosen to be Spokesman for the president of the 32nd session of the General Assembly, and spent the next three months watching from a unique vantage point the workings of that behemoth among international bodies. Looking at the earth from a circling satellite would not, I imagine, be a dissimilar experience: you saw the whole thing, but blurred by speed. There was little time to study anything in detail. But this swift and distant view proved useful when I got down to writing the TCDC book, for it had made very clear the need to look at cooperation among developing countries in a much wider perspective than is customary. There were few subjects on the vast agenda of the 32nd session that could not have been dealt with better if developing countries had more capacity to cooperate efficiently at a technical level. But I run before my horse.

Not long after the close of the 32nd session, Dr. Meguid quite unexectedly left the Conference secretariat to resume his post as Minister of Planning in Egypt. This left me more or less without guidance as to the focus of the book, and I did not seek strenuously for advisers. It was meant, I reasoned, to be an unofficial book; it was being written entirely on nights, weekends and vacations, much to the disgust of my long-suffering wife. Why not shuck the safety of "UNese" and the accepted frames of reference? The result is a book that is definitely not for specialists. It is concerned with more than traditional "development problems" and I have tried to write about fairly abstruse issues in unambiguous terms any regular reader of newspapers would understand.

A book of this sort draws upon the work of many others and to them, especially the anonymous authors of U.N. studies and reports, I owe my first bow of gratitude. Others in the first rank are Erskine Childers of UNDP, Alexandr Brychkov and Lileith Genus of CESI, and Basil Larthe of Pergamon Press. Without their encouragement and support this book would not have been possible. While the text of this book was officially "cleared" with UNDP it does not represent the views of any organization.

Introduction:
How It Began

September in New York is usually cool and clear. The haze of polluted air that hangs over the city in summer is blown away by winds that drift down from the cold Canadian north, and the sun becomes a gentle glow in lucent skies. It is undoubtedly the pleasantest time of year in the city, and the reason—beyond any weighty reasons of state—the General Assembly of the United Nations meets there then. Its annual sessions begin on the afternoon of the third Tuesday in September.

The Assembly meets at the Headquarters of the United Nations, a 16-acre plot on the eastern edge of the island of Manhattan on the shore of a tidal estuary of the Atlantic Ocean. Across the East River, as this estuary is rather inappropriately called, and downstream, are the dockyards and piers that once made New York a great harbor. But changing patterns of trade and transport have steadily lowered the vitality of the port for many years now, and the view from the United Nations across the East River is one of gray inactivity. A few tugs pull barges and ships, a few yachts and sailboats pass when the weather is nice, but the river and the waterfront on the other side have seen better days.

The Manhattan shore where the United Nations buildings stand was once a slum, a place of noisome slaughter houses and stockyards, the home of the poorest of newly arrived immigrants. The memory of this is distant now and lives only in the blank brick rear of the buildings on First Avenue across from the United Nations. The buildings are part of "Tudor City," a middle class housing complex built with its back to the river in order to save tenants the distasteful sight of the waterfront. But then in 1946 John D. Rockefeller, the American multimillionaire, donated 16 acres of the slum to the United Nations. Property values soared in the area and Tudor City is now deprived not only of a view of the water but of some of the city's most fashionable real estate.

The centerpiece of this renaissance is the 40-story U.N. Secretariat building, its green glass skin rising 550 smooth feet above First Avenue at 42nd Street. In its shadow, sloping away from the unbroken marble north facade, is the General Assembly building with its concave marble sides and shallow dome. Linking the Secretariat and the Assembly is the Conference building, part of it cantilevered out over the East River, a squat structure, housing the other major U.N. organs—the Security Council, the Economic and Social Council, the Trusteeship Council. A low-slung library building set at the south end of the site completes the complex. For the rest, the 16 acres are a stretch of neat lawns and hedges. Rows of hawthorn and sycamore, flowering cherry and dwarf fruit trees break the steady wind that comes off the river; a giant statue of a man beating a sword into a plowshare looks down on a prize-winning rose garden; ilex, myrtle and wisteria line the asphalt walks.

On the afternoon the Assembly opens, limousines with cargoes of smooth diplomats clot the curving flag-lined drive that leads through the United Nations complex. Foreign ministers and ambassadors arrive in battalions of Lincoln Continentals, Cadillacs and Mercedes Benzes; undistinguished droves of smaller cars bring first, second, and third secretaries. Newly arrived and rankless members of delegations come in taxis or walk from nearby hotels. Suprisingly enough, for all their differences in nationality, creed and color, there is a certain sameness to the professional diplomats. They are, for the most part, hard-eyed men in business suits, their shirts white or light pastels, their ties sober prints in dark colors. They exude, on this first day of the Assembly, a certain festive air as they emerge from their cars and come through the plate glass revolving doors of the delegates' entrance.

The rush begins after lunch. They stream from their cars, past the blue uniformed U.N. guards at the delegates' entrance, through the marble lobby and up the escalator, past the huge Belgian tapestry ("the string in it would go four times around the world," say U.N. guides to tourists), and onto the green carpeted area outside the Assembly Hall. The emerald carpeting continues into and across the giant oval hall, 165 feet long and 115 feet wide. At one end, the carpeting rises smoothly up two flights of steps to a magnificent podium of green marble. Behind the podium the wall looks like ancient Byzantine gold mosaic. And on either side long gold-colored slats rise in a semi-cone, like the walls of some great tepee, to a blue steel dome 75 feet above. The gold walls and the arc lamps that ring the dome create an incandescent pool around the podium. It is easy to imagine when one is on the podium that it is caught in the hot white light of a gigantic microscope. In the blaze of those lights sit the presiding officers of the Assembly, with the speaker's lectern directly beneath them. Facing them, across the fan-shaped floor of the hall, the delegates sit at their green leather-topped tables, and beyond them the floor rises in three tiers, the first tier of blue seats for

U.N. and delegation staff, brown for the press, and high in the growing gloom, a muddy green for the public. Staring down at them all from glass-fronted booths in the cobalt blue walls sit the interpreters, radio and camera technicians.

For nearly three decades now this great hall has reflected the major dramas of the world. War and pestilence, famine, flood and storm, the death of great men and the fall of empires, all have been noted in its civilized proceedings, actions in response initiated in dryly formal resolutions. Here, too, the world has looked into the future and planned for it, the eloquent idealism of the U.N. Charter translated many times in the process into the heavy prose of consensus. When the consensus is genuine it allows the gears of governments to mesh and grind into action the vast machinery that runs the modern world.

The story of this book begins with one such meshing in 1976 when on the recommendation of its Committee on Economic Affairs the General Assembly adopted a resolution[1] calling for a "United Nations Conference on Technical Cooperation among Developing Countries." In U.N. parlance it soon became the "TCDC" conference. The new acronym entered the U.N. lexicon modestly, without the clamor of controversy or the weight of organization. The world press did not particularly note its appearance nor did it generate instant recognition and excitement in the months that followed. But first impressions in this case are likely to be deceptive. TCDC probably will be a rip tide in history, a force that will reshape our world in the next few decades. This book is an attempt to explain the how and why.

One of the reasons the phrase "technical cooperation among developing countries" is often met with incomprehension or with a yawn is that people tend to interpret it in the limited sense of the "technical assistance" we have seen in the decades since World War II. That is to say, people think of technical experts and gray eminences of every stripe marching off to battle the forces of ignorance, poverty, and disease. They set up a factory here, a model farm there, contributing to the slow "development of the Third World." Meanwhile populations in the poorer countries "explode," the magnitude of their illiteracy grows every year in absolute terms, so do hunger and disease. What can TCDC imply but that greater numbers of those involved in this struggle will be brown and black and yellow? As it happens, TCDC implies a lot more. And to understand it we have to step back a bit and look at that changing picture of the past we call history.

NEW NAME FOR AN OLD PROCESS

Among the earliest evidence we have of man's capacity for conceptual thought is that found in the Stone Age remains of the "hand axe" people who lived spread out over Africa, Asia and Europe. Their "axes" were

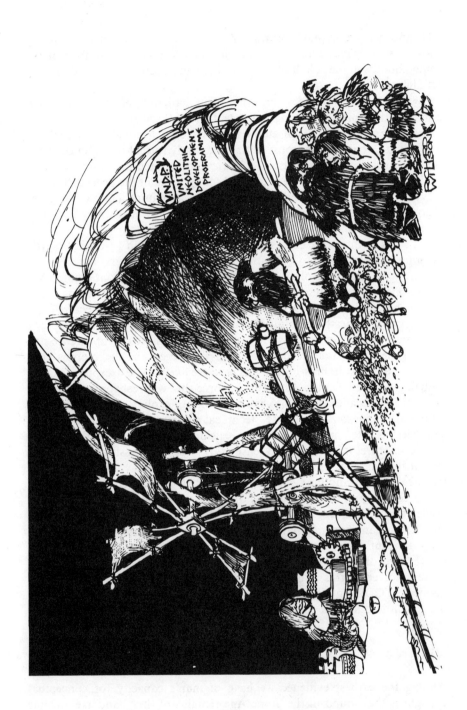

without haft or handle, mere pebbles or stone slabs chipped around the edges to produce a sharp margin and point. Yet they represented a remarkable advance in human affairs, for when we find these axes now in the south of India or England or the far tip of Africa, there is often no difference among them in form, even though they are made of quite a variety of rock. They were the first standardized tools produced by human beings, the first example we have of a concept and a technique shared by far-flung people. It is, if you will, the earliest evidence of technical cooperation for development.

Other instances are not hard to find, for societies have progressed from the stone age to the present by sharing everything from their food and clothing to their languages, ideas, and implements of war. Though this aspect of history is consistently lost in the din of armies and the noise of domination, it is undeniable. The reason is simple. Progress has always been the exception rather than the general rule among peoples, and societies have advanced to the extent they learned from the exceptions. This is not to say, of course, that the process of learning and sharing was either peaceful or simple. All manner of things could and did complicate matters. To take a rather simple example, when the potter's wheel first came into use in the village settlements of Mesopotamia, it did not immediately revolutionize the industry. People continued to make pots by a variety of more laborious ways (as they still do), because investment in a wheel required a certain minimum demand for pots. Away from the points where populations were concentrated there was not enough demand. Only in the areas where agriculture had developed enough to support an adequate population do we find today the evidence of wheel-made pottery from those early days.

Then again there are examples when a society learned something from another, and the result was disastrous. The humble stirrup originated in India, went with Buddhism to China and from there was carried to Europe. In India and China the stirrup served only the convenience of the rider. In Europe its impact was extraordinary. "Few inventions have been so simple as the stirrup, but few have had so catalytic an effect on history," says a modern European writer,[2] and he does not exaggerate. For the stirrup served to weld horse and rider into a unit, allowing a cavalryman to transmit the power of his horse, through a spear, onto an enemy. Shock combat led to the use of progressively heavier armor, the huge cost of which lay ever more oppressively on the horseless many. Upon the imported stirrup rose the power of European chivalry, and for ten centuries it remained in the feudal saddle until another Asian import, gunpowder, unseated it.

If we ask why the stirrup had the effect it did in Europe but not in Asia we are faced with philosophical complexity. Speculation on the subject is fascinating, but in the end we must admit ignorance: the values of societies can have deep and unsuspected roots. The question does point to the fact, however, that when we speak of technical cooperation among societies we

must consider more than tools and materials. When a new food comes into use in a society it is more than a source of nutrition; it can be, as the potato was in Ireland, a shaping force of history. A new concept of the social order can generate or control powerful forces; a new system of management can wreck civilizations or make deserts bloom; new modes of civic behavior can eradicate diseases and raise or lower the growth rates of populations. With every aspect of the interaction among societies we must consider the matter of values, economic, social, and political.

If the processes involved are so broad, including both physical and intellectual interaction among societies, the question might well be asked, "Why group them under the term 'technical cooperation'?" The answer is that societies can interact only as far as their technical capacity allows them to. If they do not have the means for intellectual communication, if their people and goods cannot overcome the natural and man-made barriers setting them apart, their influences on each other are necessarily limited. Such is the case now among the developing countries of Africa, Asia, and Latin America. The bridging of their diversity is the subject matter of TCDC.

List of Acronyms

CANA	Caribbean News Agency
CESI	Centre for Economic and Social Information
CIA	Central Intelligence Agency
CMEA	Council for Mutual Economic Assistance
DAC	Development Assistance Committee
EEC	European Economic Community
EFTA	European Free Trade Association
ESCAP	Economic and Social Commission for Asia and the Pacific
FAO	Food and Agricultural Organization
GATT	General Agreement on Tariffs and Trade
GDP	Gross domestic product
ILO	International Labour Organization
IPF	Indicative Planning Figure
INRES	Information Referral System
IBRD	International Bank for Reconstruction and Development
ICP	International Comparison Project
IFAD	International Fund for Agricultural Development
IMF	International Monetary Fund
ITO	International Trade Organization
MFN	Most Favored Nation
NIEO	New International Economic Order
OAU	Organization for African Unity
OECD	Organization for Economic Cooperation and Development
OEEC	Organization for European Economic Cooperation
OPEC	Organization of Petroleum Exporting Countries
SELA	Latin American Economic System
SUNFED	Special U.N. Fund for Economic Development
TCDC	Technical Cooperation among Developing Countries
UNCTAD	U.N. Conference on Trade and Development
UNDP	U.N. Development Program
UNIDO	U.N. Industrial Development Organization
World Bank	(International Bank for Reconstruction and Development)

1

Global Patterns

It has been estimated that if all the time since life began on earth were reduced to the scale of a single year, the human species would appear on the scene only at the 20th hour of the last day.[1] The later stone age would begin five minutes before midnight and our modern period would be the barest flicker at the end. Looked at in this perspective, it is apparent that civilization is a very new model for organizing life. By nature it is an experimental model and has changed constantly to adapt to external circumstances and internal demands. The different forms that evolved in different parts of the world have interacted over the centuries in many diverse ways; but till the modern period this has always been a slow process, especially with societies far removed from each other. Today, in contrast, change is transmitted across great distances with little difficulty and the pace of change in every area of life is without precedent in history. The result is the beginning of the first truly global model of civilization.

In recent years the trends contributing to global change have received a great deal of attention. It is increasingly evident that if a global model is not to result in the large scale destruction both of the natural environment and the quality of human life, it will have to outgrow the patterns set during the last phase of world history. Existing systems of production, distribution, consumption, management and power are inefficient and undemocratic. Underlying this is one of the primary factors of change today, the growth and distribution of the world population. More than three billion people live today in Africa, Asia and Latin America. About a billion others live in Europe (including the USSR), North America and Oceania. The three billion are mostly poor; the others are, in different degrees, rich. The two groups are growing at different rates, and over the next century this will cause a number of significant changes in the way the world is constituted and run. The extent to which economic and social policies are sensitive to these changes, and to the material and spiritual needs of people, will

1

determine the quality of the first global model of civilization. The care with which the new model is incorporated into that thin band of life we call the earth's ecosystem will determine whether it will survive.

Attempts to predict population growth are risky. "World population has just passed through the most dynamic quarter century in its history," says a 1978 U.N. report.[2] "Consequently it enters an end of the century period marked by enormous uncertainty with regard to long-term prospects. Vital trends by region have been departing from known precedents in such historically novel ways that judgments about the decades ahead have become uniquely risky." With this caveat the report projects world population growth as follows:

Table 1.1 Populations by Regions—1950, 1975, 2000
(in millions; medium variant)

	World	Africa	America[1]	Northern America[1]	Latin America
1950:	2501.2	218.8	330.0	166.1	163.9
1975:	3967.9	401.3	560.9	236.8	324.1
2000:	6254.4	813.7	916.1	296.2	619.9

	Asia[2,3]	East Asia[2]	South Asia[3]	Europe[2,3]	Oceania[1]	USSR
1950:	1367.7	674.8	692.9	392.0	12.6	180.1
1975:	2256.2	1006.4	1249.8	473.1	21.3	255.1
2000:	3637.3	1370.0	2267.3	539.5	32.7	315.0

[1]Hawaii, a state of the United States of America, is included in Northern America rather than Oceania.
[2]Excluding the USSR, shown separately.
[3]The European portion of Turkey is included with South Asia rather than Europe.

These figures represent a dramatic lowering of growth projections made as recently as 1976. A growing number of indicators now point to a deceleration of growth, breaking a trend that has lasted some 200 years. Despite the slowing, however, population is expected to double some time in the next century, with most of the growth concentrated in the developing countries of Africa, Asia and Latin America. Among the salient points of change in the next 25 years will be:

Rapid Increase in Number of States with Large Populations. In 1975 seven countries had populations of over 100 million. Four of them were developing countries: China, India, Indonesia and Brazil. The other three were the USSR, the United States and Japan. By the year 2000 the developing countries on the list will be joined by Nigeria, Mexico, Bangladesh and Pakistan. China and India will be mammoth states of over a billion people. Most of the states with populations over 50 million will also be developing countries: Ethiopia, Egypt, and Zaire in Africa; Colombia in Latin America; the Republic of Korea, Burma, the Philippines, Vietnam, Thailand and Turkey in Asia.

Large Number of States with Small Populations. Today, despite a quarter century of very rapid population growth there are over 80 territories with populations of less than 5 million. About half of these have less than one million people. Most of these are and will be developing countries in the year 2000.

Size of Labor Force. The dramatic decline in the death rate in developing countries is expected to continue, raising life expectancy by about 20 years over the 1950 figure (see table 1.2). The size of the working age population (between 15 and 64) will thus expand swiftly from the 1950 figure of 703 million to 1907 million by the end of the century (see table 1.3). In the developed countries, meanwhile, life expectancy is expected to increase only marginally. The population on the average will be older than now, and the number of working age people will have increased from the 1950 figure of 397 million to 639 million.

Table 1.2 Life Expectancy

	1950–1955	1970–1975	1995–2000
Developing countries	41.6	52.2	62.6
Developed countries	65.	71.1	73.4
World	46.7	55.2	64.1

Source: United Nations

Table 1.3 Estimated Labor Force Size (millions)

	1950	1975	2000
Developing countries	703	1126	1907
Developed countries	397	520	639
World	1100	1646	2536

Source: United Nations

Migration Patterns. Over the last quarter century migration patterns have broken sharply with long established trends. From the 19th century till the early 1950s Europe was the main region from which migrants originated. They went mainly to North America and Oceania. Since the mid-1950s this pattern has been broken and migrant flows have been coming from and going to new places. Emigration from Europe as a whole seems to have ceased: net movements since 1970 may even reflect a reverse trend (see table 1.4). Within Europe there have been substantial movements of workers from the poorer southern states to the north and west. There has also been a movement of people from developing countries to North America and very recently to the oil-rich states of West Asia and North Africa. Within Eastern Europe too there has been a tendency in recent years to deal with labor shortages by importing workers from other countries.

European migration patterns have changed more than direction. Until very recently the main trend was a movement of European families who wanted to settle abroad. During the last two decades the trend has changed radically and now the movement is mainly of single men who seek only to work abroad, not to settle. Surveys and statistics show that the dominant aspiration of these migrants is to return home within a year or two, a desire increased perhaps by the fact that in many host countries they live in an unreceptive social environment and are discouraged from bringing their families and settling permanently.

Table 1.4 Estimated Numbers of Immigrants from Developing Areas to Selected Developed Countries, 1960 and 1974 (in thousands)

Region of origin	Total		Northern America and Oceania[a]		Northern and Western Europe[b]	
	1960	1974	1960	1974	1960	1974
Total	3,250	9,475	2,150	5,300	1,100	4,175
Africa	525	1,900	50	200	475	1,700
Asia	925	3,725	525	1,700	400	2,025
Latin America	1,775	3,800	1,550[c]	3,350[c]	225	450
Oceania[d]	25	50	25	50	—	—

[a]Australia, Canada, New Zealand and the United States of America.

[b]Austria, Belgium, France, Federal Republic of Germany, Luxembourg, the Netherlands, Sweden, Switzerland and the United Kingdom.

[c]Including Puerto Rican immigrants in the United States of America.

[d]Other than Australia and New Zealand.

Source: *World Population Trends and Policies: 1977 Monitoring Report,* Vol. I, United Nations publication, table 147.

The attitude of the receiving countries results from their desire for unskilled workers who can be laid off in the event of an economic slowdown with a minimum of social disruption. Foreign workers can also be refused entry into the country or repatriated without much dislocation. This easy mobility would be lost if the workers were accompanied by families. The economic benefits of such policies, however, have had social costs in the form of increased crime and racial conflict.

Migration trends are impossible to project because they can and are altered by state policies, but it would be safe to say that in highly industrialized regions with slowly growing populations acute labor shortages are probable. Whether this will be met by importing labor or exporting jobs remains to be seen. The developing countries will in future have more than 80% of the world's labor force.

Urban Growth. In 1950 the urban population of industrialized countries was almost double that of developing countries. In 1975 they were about equal, between 750 and 800 million. By the year 2000 the cities in developing countries will have some 750 million more people than cities in developed countries.

The stark contrasts these trends show between the industrially developed countries of the "North" and the predominantly agrarian countries of the "South" are significant. They differentiate the world for some time to come between the North and the South, not because of any unavoidable conflict of interest, but because the two areas will need markedly different types of economic and social policies. The rates at which populations grow affect every aspect of life, whether it be food supply or employment, income distribution, the status of women, or the rights of children. The need for differentiation in policy becomes even clearer if we consider a few other statistics.

During the past three decades, the world's productive capacity has been utilized to an extent without precedent in history. Because of this, per capita incomes increased in real terms despite population growth, at the rate of 3.2% per year in the developed countries and at the somewhat lower rate of 2.6% in developing countries. World exports grew annually by 11.3%, world agricultural production by 2.7% and world industrial output by 6%. By any standards this is an undeniably impressive record. But aggregates are deceptive. If we break down the figures to see who got what, the hollowness of the impression of overall progress is immediately apparent. In 1975, out of the estimated world gross output of $6,207 billion, developed market economy countries generated $4,079 billion or 65.7%. The centrally planned economies generated $1,265 billion or 20.4%. Developing countries generated the remaining $863 billion or 13.9%. It is even more striking to put these figures in relation to the size of the populations in each of these groups.

Other figures point the same way. The share of developing countries in international trade is still no more than 25%. A mere 10% of the world's industrial output and 35% of its agricultural output originates in the developing countries. Only a modest 4% of the new international liquidity created between 1970 and 1974 is estimated to have accrued to developing countries. Staggering gaps divide the two groups of countries, not merely on the score of per capita incomes, but also on other indicators of well-being. Between 1972 and 1974, per capita daily food supplies amounted to 3,380 kilocalories or 95 grams of proteins in the developed countries, and 2,210 kilocalories or 57 grams of proteins in the developing countries. The per capita consumption of cotton, wool and man-made fibers in 1974 was 16.6 kilograms in the developed and 3.1 kilograms in the developing countries.

As we approach the end of the century we see on the one hand the evolution of systems and technologies that tend to make of the world a "global village." But it is not likely to be a very pleasant or a peaceful village if present trends are not changed. The world community is committed, at least on paper, to change them. To understand why cooperation among developing countries is a crucial element in doing so it is necessary to see how the present situation has evolved. We do this in the next chapters.

2

"Development"

Among the 150 members of the United Nations, 121 are in the category of "developing" countries. During the last three decades international usage has allowed these countries to be called "backward," "undeveloped," "underdeveloped" and "less developed." The present fashion is merely to characterize them as upwardly mobile, as "developing," or to refer to them as the "Third World" or the "South." This uneasy semantic shuffle is mainly a reflection of discomfort with broadly condescending labels, but it also points obliquely to the lack of agreement about the causes, concepts and cures relevant to "underdevelopment." As to causes, theories have ranged from the climatic (hot, tropical areas breed poverty) to the religious (the Judeo-Christian tradition is necessary for development) to the racial (Europeans developed by virtue of being European). More respected explanations are based on economic and political history. The explanation most favored by the developing countries traces the prime causes of modern poverty to the processes associated with the recent colonial period of world history.

Before the period of modern European colonialism, the centers of world affluence were in Asia and northern Africa: the Mamaluke and Ottoman empires, India and China. Their trade with Europe was conducted on terms determined by their own needs, and it reflected a substantial disinterest in anything European—except gold. Efforts to diversify European exports to Asia, which was the main source of high-quality manufactured goods and raw materials, were largely unsuccessful. When, for instance, ambassadors from England's King George III came to negotiate a trade agreement with China, their gifts, or sales samples as we would call them now, were received rather grudgingly. "The various articles presented by you, O King," said Ch'ien-lung in his reply to George, "are accepted this time by my special order to the office in charge of such functions, considering that the offerings have come from a long distance with sincere good wishes. . . . We have never set much store on strange or ingenious objects, nor do we need any of

8

your country's manufactures. . . ." It was the same in India. When Vasco da Gama presented the King of Calicut with striped cloth, hats, strings of coral, beads, wash basins and jars of oil and honey, they were accepted, but with laughter. The British East India Company, too, had trouble finding a market for its goods in India. It tried woolen cloth (Britain's staple export then), mirrors, glassware, sword blades, and lead. To popularize the last item the company even sent out plumbers to convert Indians to the use of lead pipes. But all to no avail. The Company's agents concluded that "no commodity brought out is staple enough to provide cargo for one ship."

Despite the fact that the only European commodity in demand was gold, the Asian trade grew, and competition for its considerable profits led to the discovery of the Americas. That discovery and the pillage of ancient American civilizations that followed, provided Europe with a plentiful flow of gold which financed a great expansion of European activities in Africa and Asia. The consequent flow of wealth from all these continents to Europe made possible the enormous investments necessary for what has come to be known as the Industrial Revolution. Meanwhile, processes were being initiated in the colonial territories that led them in the opposite direction, toward deindustrialization and underdevelopment. Colonial rule in Africa, Asia, and the Americas created conditions that made healthy development impossible. This happened as a matter of deliberate policy, for the primary interest of the colonial ruler was profit, not the welfare of the colonized people. The exploitation of colonized territories went hand in hand with attitudes of racial arrogance and contempt for local traditions and institutions. The resulting economic and social policies wreaked immeasurable damage in material and intellectual terms.

For example, the encouragement of cash crops such as sugar, jute, indigo, and cotton in place of food met the needs of European industries for raw materials, but it left the populations of the colonies ever more vulnerable. The consequences were grim: during the 200 years that the British were in India, the country suffered the worst series of famines in its millennial history.[1] After one of the worst of these, the great Bengal famine of 1770, when more than a third of the population died, the East India Company recorded it as a positive achievement that the land revenue it collected had increased.[2]

Industries were actively discouraged in the colonies, except for those necessary to extract raw materials and transport them to ports. Colonial educational systems virtually ignored science and technology, emphasizing skills necessary to support the administration of foreign rule. The net result of such atrocious policies was "underdevelopment" and the much discussed "gap" between industrialized countries and the rest of the word.

Not surprisingly, apologists for the affluent countries have not rushed to embrace this explanation. Daniel Moynihan, former United States Ambassador to the United Nations and perhaps the most publicized apologist in recent years, has been vehement in his disagreement. He dismissed the analysis as a half-baked ideological product of graduates from the London School of Economics (from where, he quaintly believes, leaders of developing countries get most of their ideas). According to Moynihan, tracing underdevelopment to the colonial period is merely an attempt to impute guilt to the affluent and thus backmail them into parting with more aid. However, neither Moynihan nor any other critic has been able to offer a convincing alternative explanation for the distribution of global wealth and poverty. Nor have their prescriptions to end poverty been successful in changing systems that have retarded development and are undeniably the heritage of the colonial era. Yet, because their ideas represent the interests of wealth and power, international action for over three decades has been shaped by them.

Among the most influential concepts that have shaped development policies during the last 30 years have been W.W. Rostow's ideas about economic "take-off."[3] According to this theory, development is a five-stage process whereby "traditional societies" pass through a "transition period" to the "take-off stage," reach "maturity" and become "consumer societies" on the pattern of the industrialized countries today. According to Rostow, all poor countries are at the first two stages of development and they all have trouble at the "take-off" stage because of the great social and economic transformations necessary for free flight. Not only are all existing differences of history, culture, tradition, population, resources, and institutions submerged in this theory, but poor societies today are assumed to be comparable to preindustrial Britain. The indicators that mark the rites of passage to maturity are deemed the same for all societies, as are the mechanisms of development.

As in Rostow's theory, so in all others that have influenced international development activities in the postwar period, it was assumed that poor countries would follow naturally in the footsteps of the rich. The more accommodating theorists allowed that the Third World should "learn from the mistakes of the rich," but basically they were to pass through the same stages to the same valhalla of a consumer society. In the process they were, in theory at least, to be assisted by transfers of money and technology from rich countries, as well as by a "trickling down" of growth as the rich got richer. How this "trickle" was to reach poor areas was never specified; it was supposed to happen by the operation of "market forces."

Attempts to discover laws and indices of development common to all the protean diversity of the world's poverty did, however, spawn a number of tortured abstractions and much surreal jargon. The concepts of GNP and per capita income reigned supreme for some time, both being taken as indicators of development. Countries with per capita incomes below $250 were considered "traditional societies"; those with incomes ranging up to $500 were pigeonholed "transitional." The figures were, of course, always stated in dollars, without allowance for, or even reference to, the purchasing power of local currencies.

Such conceptual muddle has kept international development efforts at the mercy of unpredictable changes in intellectual fashions. These fashions originate not from developing countries but from institutions in rich countries, and they were popularized by a network of bilateral and multilateral aid agencies with the necessary financial clout. Mahbub ul Haq, writing from his experience as a development planner in Pakistan, summed it up in a recent book. "Planners are often willing victims of these changing fashions, partly because they must keep up-to-date in the chase of development and partly because they may end up with very little foreign assistance if they do not subscribe to the currently fashionable thinking in the donor countries." He lists the following shifts to illustrate the point:

1948–55:	Import substituting industries are the key to development.
1960–65:	Import substitution is no good; export expansion is the answer.
1966–67:	Industrialization is an illusion; rapid agricultural growth is the only answer.
1967–68:	Give top priority to population control policies as all development is likely to be submerged by population explosion.
1971–75:	The poor masses have not gained much from development. Reject GNP growth; distribution must come ahead of growth.

In the 1970s the international debate on development has been forced from the dim comforts of academe into the ruder world of politics. As a result, some of its more cherished abstractions have failed to survive. The talk is now about meeting "basic needs," and strategies for "direct attacks" on poverty. The universal relevance of Northern patterns of development is being questioned and it is interesting to consider why.

The reassessment has not come because a great light suddenly dawned upon development economists, clarifying the real needs of the poor. On the contrary, a convincing argument can be made that their new insights resulted from a recognition of the real needs of the very rich. During the last decade two specters have been raised over the industrial world—resource shortages and environmental pollution. These are seen as definite threats to the quality of life, the political structures, and the position of economic elites in affluent countries. If poorer countries followed in the footsteps of the rich, it would exacerbate both the environmental and the resource problems. Hence "basic needs."

Another discovery of recent vintage is that all talk of "closing the gap" between rich and poor countries is unrealistic. Robert McNamara, President of the World Bank, spelled this out to the Bank's Board of Governors in 1977.

The algebra of closing the absolute gap in per capita incomes can be summarized as follows: a poor country growing faster than a rich one will not begin to reduce the absolute income gap between them until the inverse ratio of their growth rates is equal to the ratio of their per capita incomes. Thus, if the historical growth rates continue into the future, the present absolute income gap will continue to widen since developed and developing countries have been experiencing similar rates of per capita growth in the last 25 years. Even if developing countries manage to double their per capita growth rate, while the industrial world maintains its historical growth, it will take nearly a century to close the absolute income gap between them. Among the fastest growing developing countries, only 7 would be able to close the gap within 100 years, and only another 9 within 1000 years.

Based on this figuring, Mr. McNamara told the Governors that "closing the gap was never a realistic objective. . . . Given the immense differences in the capital and technological base of the industrialized nations as compared with that of the developing countries, it was simply not a feasible goal. Nor is it one today."

Reflecting this discovery, the World Bank has begun to come up with studies and statistics that show that the gap between poor and rich is not as wide as we might think. The Bank's International Comparison Project (ICP), for instance, has related the local purchasing power of currencies in a number of countries to show that the poor are really not all that poor. The purchasing power of the rupee in India, for instance, when related to the purchasing power of the dollar in the United States, produces a higher per capita income for Indians than traditional statistics allow. Cosmetically, then, the gap between Indians and Americans is narrowed. Meanwhile, the "basic needs" approach focuses on the "absolute poor," who, the Bank asserts, will be with us into the next century. Thus, neatly, the focus of attention is shifted from the North-South relationship to the internal situation in developing countries.

Another discovery of past irrelevance comes from an American academic, Dennis A. Rondinelli, the author of a study titled "International Assistance Policy and Development Project Administration: The Impact of Imperious Rationality."[4] Commenting on the many requirements of planning administrative procedure imposed upon poor countries, Mr. Rondinelli comments:

> Perhaps the ultimate irony is that many developing countries have been judged backward, inefficient, and defective in public planning and administration because they cannot apply analytical and management systems techniques, the efficacy and practicality of which remain unproven even in advanced industrialized nations.... Studies of weapons systems projects in the United States, in which many of the management techniques now prescribed for developing countries were conceived, indicate that ... scheduling and control procedures gave a "myth of managerial effectiveness" to project administration without contributing to substantive results.

The result, in the words of a planner from a developing country, is that:

> Projects requiring foreign aid must be packaged with a view to finding a "buyer." This takes the form of window dressing. It is the general feeling in most developing countries that the more technical and complex the presentation, the more the use of shadow prices, tradeoffs, engineering coefficients, convincing evaluation of investment criteria, the better the chances of finding a bilateral or multilateral donor.[5]

When we consider the literature of development during the last 30 years it is surprising that a reassessment of basic assumptions took so long and that it had to come the way it did. Why did anyone ever accept the theory that countries in Africa, Asia and Latin America, with widely varying histories and cultures, with different social structures, geographies and resources, could follow the same path to prosperity as that taken by European countries a century earlier? Especially when this belief was unfounded in anything but the most superficial analysis of what had happened in Europe? And how did this belief prevail over critics as significant as Mahatma Gandhi in India and others elsewhere who wanted development in indigenously direct ways? A full answer to these questions would—and should—take a book. Suffice it to say that it is a reflection of the intellectual dependency that has characterized poverty in the post-colonial period. It could not have happened so easily if poor countries had the technical capacity for consultation and action in the area of development. The ideas of Gandhi could not have been dismissed so easily if those in the North who determine the currency of fashionable ideas had not branded him an irrelevant mystic luddite. And during the last 30 years more ideas would certainly have emerged from the Southern experience with development if existing filters were not so successful in removing them.

In the next chapter we consider the creation of exclusive Northern systems—the bases of wealth and power in the world.

3

Rich Men's Clubs

Among the many miracles of modern times is the economic cooperation that rebuilt and reshaped the world after the last great war. Focused around two groups of countries, one capitalist, the other socialist, this cooperative effort inaugurated and sustained for three decades the most productive period of human economic history. But the benefits of their cooperation eluded a third group—the developing countries. Africa, Asia and Latin America, with more than two-thirds the world population and a great wealth of raw material resources, had no part in creating the instruments of postwar cooperation. Consequently they found themselves with little control or use of these instruments, and without power to influence events of crucial importance to their well-being. Today, a generation after World War II, these developing countries are moving to remedy their disadvantage and create a more equitable global order. In doing so they seek to create among themselves the means for cooperation necessary to protect their interests and bargain on equal terms within the various clubs the rich have organized to run the world. To understand this process it is necessary, once again, to consider the past as prologue. Why have industrially developed countries acted as they have? What structures and what ideas hold them together and exclude the rest?

THE PAST AS PROLOGUE

The period between the First and Second World Wars saw vast and turbulent changes in the international order. Many of these changes had disastrous effects on prosperous states, and the experience conditioned the thinking of those who planned the global order after World War II. Twice in a generation they had seen economic rivalries lead to war; many times they saw economic policies substitute for war. In planning a new world system they sought as a matter of high priority to prevent a recurrence of this pattern and create a system that would encourage generally beneficial economic policies.

In doing this, the efforts of planners focused on two areas—trade and monetary affairs. The two areas have been historically interlinked, since the use of money evolved as a means of easing the rigidities of barter, but it was only in the late colonial period that the linkage produced problems with major economic and social implications. In precolonial days trade was comparatively limited, involving mostly the exchange of luxury goods. Values were set by the circumstances of individual traders. During the colonial period the volume and nature of trade changed: there was growing demand for raw materials, goods such as cotton, sugar, jute, tobacco and tea. These were exchanged for industrial manufactures. Advances in technology allowed bulk shipments, making possible such outlandish exchanges as ice from America for Indian tea.

The point to be noted is that the unprecedented growth in diversity and volume of trade began to affect societies in basic ways. The new industrial structures of Europe were built on this trade and its economics thus assumed crucial importance to them. Consequently, the problem of how to set standards of exchange for goods and currencies became, and still remains, one of the primary concerns of national policy.

Within the colonial empires, of course, the problems were easily solved—the colonies having no voice in defense of their own interests. Among the empires of Europe the problems assumed disruptive proportions only when competition intensified for export markets and Germany, a disgruntled latecomer on the imperial scene, began challenging the dominance of others. The animosities thus engendered led to World War I and the loss of fiscal Eden in the form of the Gold Standard. Governments met the vast expenses of war by ignoring the cardinal rule of the Gold Standard system—that money be issued only when fully backed by gold reserves. The system broke down and the result was domestic inflation and international confusion about the relative values of currencies. The orderly, fixed rate of exchange among currencies which the gold standard had enforced, became impossible. Exchange rates became a matter of government discretion and their actions, reflecting intense national rivalries, came to be called "beggar thy neighbour" policies. Europe passed into a period of economic anarchy as governments tried to gain advantages in trade without regard to the effect on their trading partners. Manipulation of currency exchange rates became routine.

To protect national industries from the effects of such policies, governments set up high tariff barriers, imposed quotas and other restrictions that had a disastrous impact on trade. Periods of booming demand and inflation were followed by painful recessions. People in the export-import business were unsure from day to day whether government policies would ruin them or make them rich. Such uncertainty led to shrinking trade and ultimately to the collapse of all world markets, in a sequence now remembered as the Great Depression. The processes of recovery saw more economic warfare. "Each successive disturbance accelerated the drift to self-sufficiency, isolation and impoverishment until finally the have nots resorted to armed aggression on the plea of economic self defence," notes a recent commentator.[1] Predictably and inexorably Europe's economic battles led to World War II.

Meanwhile the Soviet Union had emerged from World War I as a socialist state and set itself on a different but equally difficult course, struggling in a hostile international environment to industrialize a poor agrarian society. The concepts and means employed in the centrally planned Soviet economy were different from those elsewhere but here, too, the experiences of the interwar years moulded the thinking of those who sought to create a new order. Neither among the capitalist countries nor in the socialist group were the bitter enmities of the war allowed to hinder cooperation for development. Countries of considerable diversity in size, population and power joined to create the institutions and systems beneficial to the group.

Of the two, the capitalist grouping has been, and continues to be, of greater relevance to the developing countries. This is not only a heritage from the colonial period, but because the concepts and patterns of socialist development, formulated as they were during the cold war, eschewed major involvement with economies outside the group. In recent years concerted efforts have been made to expand the links of socialist countries with others, but the focus of attention for poor countries still remains the capitalist systems.

THE CAPITALIST SYSTEMS

In the summer of 1944, when it no longer took an astrologer to predict how World War II would end, the "United and Associated Nations" set about deciding the shape of the world to come. Among the most important steps in this process was a meeting held at Bretton Woods in the American state of New Hampshire. There, at the luxurious Mount Washington Hotel ($11 per day with all meals) about 700 delegates from 44 countries met for the United Nations Monetary and Financial Conference. For most of the month of July these delegates hammered out agreements on a monetary stabilization fund and an investment bank. The first became the IMF (the International Monetary Fund). The second took the form of the International Bank for Reconstruction and Development, generally called the World Bank. A third element, an international trade organization proposed as part of the Bretton Woods System was never created. This omission, as much as the two organizations that were established, would decide how the world's market economy system developed in the next decades.

The participants at Bretton Woods were not equals. Most of Europe was still occupied territory. The French, for instance, were mentioned in conference documents not as the representative of France but as the "French Delegation." They felt their interests were being ignored, and the head of the delegation, Mendes-France, was moved at one point to exclaim: "And how will it look when I come back to my people and explain to them 'I went some months ago to Bretton Woods and explained our position. I told them, we want this, this, and this and in all these questions I have to tell you I come with zero.' "

The British were in a better position because their delegation was led by the widely respected economist, Maynard Keynes, who had been involved from the beginning in the formulation of proposals for the conference. However, they, too, were without power. For the previous three years Britain had been kept from bankruptcy and defeat by the American lend-lease program, and Britian hoped for more aid after the war.

The Soviet delegation had power, as acknowledged in formal arrangements. But the Russians did not speak English and, noted one observer, "neither did their interpreters." They also had trouble getting Moscow to respond to the various proposals and arrangements. As a result the Russian delegates were inordinately cautious. When a Russian was elected to chair a major committee he immediately turned over the job to his Canadian deputy.

The countries of Africa, Asia, and Latin America counted for even less. They were then, as now, in a majority: 26 of the 44 countries present. But only three were African (Egypt, Ethiopia, and Liberia) and five Asian (China, India, Iran, Iraq, and the Philippines). Of these India was still a British colony, the Philippines an American "Commonwealth," and the others had all experienced the brusque exercise of imperial power to settle any show of independence. So too had the 18 Latin American countries present, as the Mexican delegate acknowledged when he asked bitterly why it was necessary to propose that rich countries be given the formal contractual power to change the gold value of currencies of poor countries. "Why should we ask small countries to participate in decisions which probably will be made, as they have always been made in the past, without their consent?" he asked.

There was also the problem of tactics and planning. The small delegations from poor countries—in the case of Guatemala the "delegation" was a single post graduate economics student from Harvard—were no match for the numerous and carefully prepared delegates from the country that planned and dominated the Bretton Woods conference—the United States. The Americans knew precisely what they wanted from Bretton Woods. In a pamphlet titled "The Bretton Woods Proposals: Questions and Answers" the United States Treasury Department spelled it out:

It has been estimated that our exports, which were only three billion dollars in 1938, will have to be more than tripled in the post-war period if we are to achieve full employment of manpower and full utilization of our enormously expanded industrial capacity.

Exchange control is not the only obstacle the American exporter has had to fight, again and again he has had his foreign markets for automobiles, radios, tools, tobacco, lard, cotton and grain cut from under him by currency devaluation and the manipulation of exchange rates. This is the way it worked; if payment was customarily made in the currency that was devalued, American exporters were no longer able to sell in that country except at higher prices in terms of the devalued currency, of if payment was customarily made in dollars, foreigners who might otherwise buy our goods found the price of dollar exchange purchased with devalued currency prohibitive. In either case if the American exporter was to continue to do business in that country, he had to be content with reduced dollar proceeds, which meant cutting costs, and that meant cutting wages.

If in any event he could not hold the market, he had to cut production, and that meant cutting jobs.

. . .Each country would want to assure itself of necessary imports by entering into two way agreements with other countries. The smaller countries would seek protective ties with the larger . . . with trading areas narrowly limited, countries like the United States would suffer most. A restricted volume of foreign trade would mean, as it did in the 1930s, that large surpluses of many goods would have to be dumped on the home market. The consequences would be depressed prices, foreclosures, and unemployment.

It is generally agreed that an increasingly large volume of foreign investment by the United States is essential to our own economic security. Without it we cannot expect to build up the volume of exports required to help absorb the output of our greatly expanded industrial plant.

MONEY

These interests were reflected in the Articles of Agreement of the IMF. The 20 Articles were, and still are, difficult for nonspecialists to interpret, but their main purpose was to create a code of conduct for countries. U.S. Assistant Secretary of State Dean Acheson provided as succinct a layman's summary as any when he said:

There are four things . . . that the Agreement provides, which shall be followed by the members of the Fund.
First of all, the members are asked to:
   (a) Define their currencies in terms of gold.
   (b) Keep its currency within 1 per cent of that determined value.
   (c) Undertake not to restrict current transactions in their currency. Not to place restrictions on the purchase and sale of services, so far as their currency is concerned. After the post-war transition that will, at one stroke, do away with this whole vast system of exchange control, by which any person in a country who wishes to buy something from abroad must go to his Government to get the Government's permission to buy that article.
   (d) If it became necessary, in your opinion, at some later time to change the value of your currency . . . you must get the consent or agreement of the Fund to do this. You may change your currency without the consent of the Fund but only after consultation with the Fund for minor changes aggregating 10 per cent.

What Acheson did not mention was a matter of critical importance. The conference had put the dollar next to gold at the center of the new monetary system. The par value of a member's currency, said the IMF Agreement, shall be expressed "in terms of gold and U.S. dollars." As the United States then held some 66 percent of the world's monetary gold, the dollar was, in an expression popular at the time, "as good as gold." It gave the United States a great advantage, for it could "create" gold more easily than even the chief mining countries, South Africa and the Soviet Union. A Keynesian proposal that would have prevented this advantage by creating a new unit of IMF managed international currency—the Bancor—got nowhere.

Other proposals to share the U.S. advantage with silver producing countries got nowhere either. Pleading the cause of silver as a monetary metal, Antonio Espinosa de los Monteros of Mexico sounded a theme that has come to be a staple at international gatherings on economic development: the interests of the weak should not be ignored.

> The Mexican delegation is aware of the argument against recognizing silver as a component of the monetary pattern of the world. Nobody who is anybody, it is said, should give a thought to the silver problem, since it affects only the so called backward peoples of the earth, whose international trade added together is but a minor negligible fraction of the world trade. If this same or a similar attitude were to be applied to all the problems of the post-war world, it is difficult to see how the world could be happy. For how can we brush aside so lightly the economic habits of millions upon millions of humble people, just because they are poor and cannot thus "belong" amongst the elite of this earth?

The same note was struck in a statement by A.D. Shroff of India when he complained that the problem of his country's vast Sterling balance had not received the attention it deserved. During the war a bankrupt Britain had consumed on credit a great flow of Indian resources. However, the Sterling balance India thus acquired was frozen unilaterally by the British after the war; it could only be used for buying British goods once their devastated industries resumed production. India wanted the IMF Agreement to make provisions for unfreezing some portion of its assets in Britain, allowing it immediately to get badly needed imports from elsewhere. The United States opposed the idea on the grounds that it would "overload" the Fund. Shroff, after commenting that he failed to see how the Fund could be overloaded, went on: "It may be that unfortunately situated as we are politically, perhaps the 'big guns' in the conference may not attach great importance to a country like India. But I am bound to point out this: if you are prepared to ignore a country of the size of India, with four hundred million population and with natural resources not incomparable to some of the biggest powers on this earth, we cannot be expected to make our full contribution to the strengthening of the resources of the Fund." But Indian interests continued to be ignored and its Sterling balance remained frozen.

If the interests of the weak were ignored in the Bretton Woods Agreement, those of the "strong" Soviet Union fared little better. True, its proven military power and its gold mines had won a place of respect for the USSR. Its quota of subscriptions to the Fund was third in rank (after the United States and Britain), and its representative was to have one of the five permanent seats on the Board of Governors. Yet, in spite of the general expectation that it would develop into one of the great economic powers of the world, the Soviet Union found itself out of the club by the time the Governors of the IMF met for the first time in March 1946. The political atmosphere had steadily grown darker after the death of President Roosevelt in the United States and the USSR never ratified the Agreement it signed at Bretton Woods. Three days before the first IMF Governors' meeting, Britain's Winston Churchill, while on a visit to the United States, made his famous "iron curtain" speech, signaling the official excommunication of the Soviet Union. The cold war had begun and it left the U.S. without peers in the IMF, the World Bank, and the systems they supervised.

TRADE

Ideally, the Bretton Woods System should have included three elements: an international trade organization, a monetary fund, and an investment bank. The need for a trade organization was clear for prewar monetary tangles were no more than a reflection of trade war. Financial arrangements, as in the IMF, could lay the ground rules for a healthy exchange of goods and services, but a separate organization would be needed to ensure that the development of trade would be for the common good. As Sir Shanmukham Chetty of India pointed out at Bretton Woods, the first IMF article dealing with expansion and balanced growth of international trade did not mention the special needs of poor countries. The article, he said, conceived of balance as being an equality of exports and imports.

> Though this is an important aspect of balanced growth, we attach great importance also to the balanced character and composition of international trade. A predominant flow of raw materials and food stuffs in one direction and highly manufactured goods in the other direction is not a really balanced international trade from this latter point of view. It is only by greater attention to the industrial needs of countries like India that you can achieve a real and rational balance.

No attempt was made at Bretton Woods in this direction. It was left for the United Nations Conference on Trade and Employment to do so. Meeting in Havana from November 1947 to March 1948 the Havana conference did succeed in drawing up the charter of an International Trade Organization (ITO) which would, in addition to expanding trade along agreed-upon lines, "foster and assist industrial and general economic development particularly of those countries which are still in the early stages of industrial development." But in the process of agreement, the fears that Mahmoud Saleh el Falaki of Egypt had voiced at Bretton Woods proved valid. There was indeed "conflict between the interests of highly industrialized countries, and the recent tendency in certain raw material producing countries to industrialize." As a result, so many loopholes and reservations were embroidered into the draft charter of the ITO that of the 53 nations that signed the Havana Charter only two ratified it.

The General Agreement on Tariffs and Trade (GATT) resulted from the failure of the negotiations to create an ITO. While the preparatory committee for the Havana conference was laboring on the draft charter, a few governments involved in that effort agreed to sponsor negotiations to lower tariffs and other trade restrictions among themselves. The agreements that resulted were embodied in a treaty and signed in October 1947 in Geneva. It was originally accepted by 23 countries; since then the contracting parties have grown to 84. The reason the growth in membership has not been as spectacular as in other international organizations is that membership in GATT is not an unmixed blessing, especially for developing countries (see below). But it has become the only permanent international instrument governing world trade because the nations that dominate world trade find it useful.

GATT's efforts at emancipating international trade from the tangle of prewar restrictions and discriminatory practices proceeded on the basis of two main principles: reciprocity and the application of the Most Favored Nation (MFN) concept. Both have worked to the disadvantage of developing countries. Reciprocity has meant that unless a country can give a concession, it cannot get one; since their economic weakness made it difficult for developing countries to give concessions, they received scarcely any. This explains why, after nearly three decades of a steady process of dismantling tariffs under the aegis of GATT, developed countries' imports from developing ones remain typically subject to tariff restrictions. And when reductions are made, as a United Nations study[2] showed in 1968, developed countries get more of a cut. Before the "Kennedy Round" of tariff cutting talks, for instance, manufactured goods from developing countries faced an average nominal tariff rate of 17.1 percent in developed countries, compared to a rate of only 10.9 percent for manufactured goods from developed countries. After the talks the rate had dropped to 11.8 percent for developing countries but it had been lowered to 6.5 percent for developed countries. The MFN concept meant that any concessions developing countries agreed to exchange, even bilaterally, had to be extended automatically to all other GATT members, developed and developing alike. It is true that by the same token they were also recipients of tariff concessions negotiated between other members. But by and large such concessions pertained to industrial products from developed countries and few developing countries could take advantage of them.

The process begun under GATT was carried furthest by the countries which now form the European Economic Community (EEC), popularly called the Common Market. Beginning as a customs union in 1957, the members of the Common Market progressively reduced their tariff barriers, eliminating them completely in July 1968. Meanwhile they raised common barriers against the rest of the world. The aim of complete economic union by 1969 was not achieved, but considerable integration of economic structures and commercial policies made the EEC comparable and competitive with the United States. Needless to say, the Common Market has also enhanced the bargaining power of the participants in their dealings with the much less powerful economies of developing countries. Another factor has been the preservation and, in many cases, the introduction of new nontariff barriers to trade. Subsidies, quotas, restrictions on quality and other nontariff barriers are now regarded as more important than tariffs in their trade-impeding effects. Given their weak bargaining position, poorer countries suffer proportionately more from these effects.

The agreements that produced the IMF and GATT set the rules for the postwar economic game. The game itself, over the last three decades, has involved a host of other bodies, both public and private, and in the following chapters some of the most important of these are considered. To the extent that there is a centralized expression of this intricate mesh of wealth it is the Organization for Economic Cooperation and Development (OECD). Founded in 1961, the OECD replaced the Organization for European Economic Cooperation (OEEC) that had been established in 1948. The change from the OEEC to the OECD is significant in that it meant the extension of membership privileges to the wealthy of all regions —from a regional organization it has developed into one based on class.[3] Its professed aim is to "promote economic and social welfare throughout the OECD area by assisting member governments in the formulation of policies designed to this end and by coordinating these policies." It also seeks to "stimulate and harmonize its members' aid efforts in favour of developing countries." The governing body of the OECD is a Council which meets regularly at the heads-of-delegations level and once a year at the ministerial level. The Council, with a 13-member executive committee, is responsible for all questions of general policy. Most of the Organization's work, however, is done in specialized committees and working groups which number over one hundred. Among these is the Development Assistance Committee (DAC), the focal point for decisions relating to development aid. Through the work of this committee and with its collection and publication of economic statistics, the OECD exerts considerable influence on public perceptions and the policies of governments and multilateral agencies.

Links to the Poor

As all this indicates, developing countries have not been equal partners in
the postwar systems of cooperation created by developed countries with
market economies. They are, however, of critical importance to the welfare
of developed countries, both as producers of a wide range of raw materials
and as markets for manufactured goods. Reflecting this importance are a
number of market system mechanisms working for the development of the
poor countries. The most important of these is the International Bank for
Reconstruction and Development (IBRD), better known as the World
Bank. Created at the same time as the IMF, the Bank's initial purpose was
the rebuilding of war-devastated Europe. However, the introduction of the
Marshall Plan made IBRD superfluous in this area, and so it turned its
attentions to developing countries. Like the IMF, the World Bank is
completely under the control of industrialized countries at the policy and
operational levels. Its money is mostly from the capital markets of
industrialized countries and, under the Bank's charter, lending is limited to
projects that would generate a direct earnings flow sufficient to repay the
loan and interest charges. The use of all loans is controlled down to the
purchase of goods and services at the project level.

Developing countries have used the World Bank's resources but they have
not been unaware of the implications. As Amon J. Nsekela, formerly
Principal Secretary to the Treasury in Tanzania, states:

> Historically it has promoted export agriculture and the infrastructure for mineral and
> agricultural exports above all else. Until five years ago virtually all of its loans to
> Tanzania, for instance, were closely related to promoting exports and imports. Critical as
> that may be as part of a strategy, when it is the whole strategy it is not one for national
> development but rather for the development of dependent underdevelopment.

The Bank cannot, Mr. Nsekela continues,

> claim freedom from the overweening arrogance of many North Americans and Europe-
> ans and of most North Atlantic or European-centered so-called global institutions. Its
> "experts" have always "known better," even when their first need was for the most
> elementary data which an impartial observer might have supposed to be a precondition
> for forming any views on what was correct. One observed rather grandly to some of my
> colleagues: "I know what we should do in Tanzania. Of course I haven't been there yet
> but I'll be out soon and stay long enough to learn all the facts I need to know. Probably
> two weeks."

Such attitudes have begun to change in recent years, Mr. Nsekela notes, but
"in the field of trade and the related area of control over the activities of
transnational corporations the Bank has been limited both by its charter
and its dominant members."[4]

"Aid"

The World Bank is now the largest single source of external capital for some 80 developing countries. This is often referred to in the popular press as "aid" and its importance construed out of all proportion. Multilateral and bilateral aid together is estimated to constitute only about 1 to 2 percent of the resources committed by developing countries to their own development. The large bulk of this "aid" consists of loans for which interest rates are low and repayment periods long—but they are by no means gifts. In the World Bank and in the other multilateral development banks the aid is controlled by the donor group of rich countries by means of their voting strength and by "traditions" that lead to the selection of nationals from one of their countries to head the institutions. In other institutions where the rich countries do not have weighted voting advantages, they control by other means. The U.N. Development Program (UNDP) has both. Its 48-member Governing Council gives almost equal representation to developed and developing countries, despite the large majority of the latter. Control of the UNDP by the developed countries is further assured by a system of annual voluntary contributions for its funding. If policies displease the donors, purse strings can be drawn. Under such conditions "aid" is strongly supported by the business communities of the donor countries. From even a cursory look at the statistics it is easy to understand why. In an article titled "Foreign Aid Has Friends Back Home: Businessmen" (the *New York Times*, July 30, 1978), financial reporter Ann Crittenden presented some of these figures.

Multilateral assistance contracts are not as easily obtained by United States concerns as bilateral awards are. Nevertheless American companies have done fairly well, last year winning contracts worth $364 million, about 22% of the total, not counting subcontract awards. Procurements in the United States financed by the World Bank alone totaled $5 billion between 1946 and 1976. . . . In addition to direct procurement, the World Bank's supporters point out that the institution, based in Washington, spent $800 million on operations in this country between 1946 and 1976, more than the $781 million that the United States paid into the World Bank during the same period. When interest payments received by American investors from World Bank bonds are included, the American economy receives $9.50 for every $1 the United States paid into the Bank. . . . As for benefits to American banks, not only do World Bank loans make it easier for countries to service their massive debts to United States institutions but also the World Bank itself deposits most of its $5.5 billion in liquid funds in American banks. A World Bank spokesman said last week, "The American banks have had a bonanza out of this thing." From UNDP, according to one of its publicity brochures, the rate of return for the American dollar is more modest: 130 percent.

THE WORLD SOCIALIST SYSTEM

In January 1949 representatives of Bulgaria, Czechoslovakia, Hungary, Poland, Romania, and the Soviet Union met in Moscow and agreed on the need for wider economic cooperation among themselves. To achieve this, they created the Council for Mutual Economic Assistance (CMEA).[5] In large part the initiative was an attempt at collective self-reliance in the face of what the participating states considered hostile economic policies by the capitalist countries of Western Europe and North America. Thus, while the Marshall Plan revived and integrated the market economies of Western Europe, the countries to the east set about doing the same thing, albeit with different aims, principles, and methods. In the West there was a progressive reduction of customs duties, quantitative restrictions, export subsidies and limitations on the movements of capital and labor, setting the stage for private enterprise—especially transnational corporations. In the East the integrating mechanism was based above all "on an organic combination of the coordination of plans which is the basic method of organizing cooperation."[6] While many sovereign aspects of the national economies in the West were submerged to facilitate joint effort, in the East cooperation did "not involve the creation of supranational bodies."

The CMEA system is now based upon a charter adopted at Sofia a decade after the organization was founded; and its operational focus is now a "Comprehensive Program" adopted in 1971. The Program spells out in considerable detail the basic aims, principles, directions, forms, methods and measures for a 15- to 20-year period. Participants have agreed to coordinate their activities primarily within CMEA, making it the center for all forms of multilateral activity. The manner of this cooperation is detailed and specific. It is based on the "recommendations" of the main representative bodies of CMEA (Session, Executive Committee, and Commissions). These recommendations can deal with coordination of national economic plans, specialization and cooperation in production, development of industry, agriculture, and transport. A "recommendation" has legal force in that member countries must consider it and report back to the CMEA secretariat within 60 days. If a country accepts a recommendation it then becomes legally binding.

The CMEA system has had great success in developing industry and trade, and such supporting structures as transport, communications and power. Cooperation in industrialization is aimed at the "gradual drawing closer and evening out of the levels of economic development." Preferential terms of cooperation are made for the industrially less developed countries of the group, including the "choice of new branches of production for international specialization." The less industrially developed countries receive scientific and technical assistance to maintain high standards in the areas they choose and the terms of the agreement also ensure them a stable and steadily expanding market for their products. The results of such policies have been dramatic. In 1950 the CMEA group had a share of about 17 percent in the world's industrial production. They now have over 33 percent.

In trade—a state monopoly—commodities are divided into three categories. The first includes those for which long-term agreements and yearly protocols fix the quantities to be traded, as well as specific delivery terms of quality and time. This category includes basic raw materials, fuel, machinery, and equipment, agricultural commodities and food. The second category includes items for which long-term agreements and annual protocols fix only value quotas while details of delivery are settled between buyer and seller. The third category consists of items for which no quotas are fixed.

The system has been particularly successful in increasing intragroup trade. Such exchanges form a much higher proportion of the CMEA's overall foreign trade than, for instance, among EEC countries. The proportions also point to the system's main weakness: being a completely planned effort it has been easier to build trade within the group than outside it. In the monetary area, too, this disability exists, for the CMEA's "collective currency," the "transferable rouble" is not freely convertible. It is at present a valid international currency only within the CMEA group where it is, under the provisions of the group's "Comprehensive Program" "secured by commodity reserves and by the planned development of trade . . . in accordance with coordinated contractual prices fixed on the basis of world prices freed of the harmful influence exerted by the interplay of speculative forces on the capitalist market." Trade relations with developing countries have been growing in recent years, but a major constraint has been the lack of arrangements to multilateralize payments.

The development of the postwar global order has thus been marked by the growth of two systems of intense cooperation. The developing countries exist on the peripheries of both. In the next chapter we look in more detail at some other aspects of their marginalization.

4

Fortune's Very Select Few

Among the rich men's clubs that dominate the world, the most exclusive and perhaps the most powerful are giant transnational corporations. Their influence comes not only from command over capital, technology and information, but from their close alliance with the military power of their parent states. This relationship is not a new one, nor is it a recent discovery. In 1600, when Britain's Queen Elizabeth I gave a group of investors the right to be "one body corporate" in the pursuit of profit in the East Indies, the new company was more than an economic instrument. In addition to its monopoly on the East Indian trade, the company was authorized to make and enforce laws in the areas it entered. To begin with this "authority" was of course presumptuous; the East India Company traded in India as a vassal of the Moghul Emperor at Delhi, and whatever authority it had came from him. But over the years, in defending its commerce, the Company involved itself in politics and, with the help of local allies and the British navy and army, it grew in power. By 1843 the British Governor General in Bengal was in a position to stop sending the annual tribute to the Emperor at Delhi. By 1848, as British Opposition Leader Benjamin Disraeli noted in Parliament, a new system of Indian policy had begun. The Company had decided to "increase the revenue of our dominions by increasing our dominions."

Similarly, the Royal African Company, the Dutch and French East India Companies, the Hudsons Bay Company and other such enterprises pioneered colonial rule around the world with the close support of their parent countries. In doing so they presided over the creation of international systems which naturally tended to their own benefit—and, consistently, to the detriment of the colonies. Mutually beneficial relationships among the colonies themselves suffered under the new regimes. The fate of 16th century Malacca (modern Malaysia) exemplifies this process. Malacca was, according to a contemporary source, a place to which merchants came "from all over the world." The cosmopolitan population of the city included "merchants and sailors from all the lands between Arabia and China, whether Moors, Jews or heathens." Especially numerous were the "Gujeratis from Cambay, the Klings and Bengalis of the east coast of India, the men of Java, the Chinese and the 'Gores' (Japanese)."[1] But by the end of the 16th century Portuguese control of Malacca was affecting its trade. The Portuguese were driving the Japanese sailors out of the rice trade by enforcing a system of licenses for ships going east. Not surprisingly, most of the licenses went to the Portuguese.

In trade, shipping, banking, insurance; in the growing areas of science and technology; in international usage and law; in every system they replaced or created, Europeans were the controllers and main beneficiaries. There was one center for all these systems—Europe—and the periphery was the colonies.

To say that Europe was the center is not merely a figure of speech. European corporations made the decisions to produce, to buy and to sell that affected the rest of the world. London, for instance, was the "centre of the world money market" because in a small part of it known as "The City" —an area of about a square mile—were the Bank of England, the gold market, the international insurance market, the major commodity exchanges and the offices of the chief merchant banks. Supporting their activities were the world's largest fleet of merchant ships and the largest of the colonial empires. As Harry Magdoff writes:

> Until the 1880s British banks had virtually no competition in financing of international trade outside the continent of Europe. In the latter decades of the 19th century, German and French systems of foreign banks began to duplicate the spread of British banks, except in regions under the British flag. Yet, despite the growing competition, England's dominance in the financing of foreign trade persisted. In fact, in the late 19th and early 20th century most of the U.S. foreign trade—and most of international trade originating elsewhere—was financed not with dollars, but in sterling by London banks.[2]

Two world wars broke the power of Europe, but not of their systems of dominance. As Samuel P. Huntington told the Commission on the Year 2000 of the American Academy of Arts and Science:

> By the year 2000 it should be clear retrospectively that the dominant feature of international politics during the 20 years after World War II was neither the East-West confrontation between the U.S. and Sino-Soviet bloc, nor the North-South conflict between the developed and under-developed countries. Instead, the crucial relationship was that between the United States and Western Europe, and the dominant feature of international politics during this period was the expansion of the power of the United States. A crucial feature of this expansion was the extension of American power into the vacuums that were left after the decline of the European influence in Asia, Africa and even Latin America.[3]

As is usual with writers from the North, Huntington exaggerates the importance of the North. But the process he describes has been undoubtedly a significant one. What it meant, essentially, was the spectacular growth of U.S. based transnational corporations. American banks, for instance, grew not merely by setting up branches internationally but by creating subsidiary corporations which in turn bought into foreign banks, insurance houses and other financial institutions. It is interesting to see how the process was made possible by an amendment to the U.S. Federal Reserve Act 8 in 1919, as the First World War drew to a close. As late as 1950 U.S. banks operated in only 24 other countries and they had only 95 branches in all. By 1972 the number of branches had grown to over a thousand. In 1976, for example, just one U.S. bank—Citicorp—had 250 branches and affiliates abroad, 176 of them in developing countries. By 1979 the 13 largest U.S. banks were deriving almost 50 percent (in some cases over 80 percent) of their total revenues from abroad.

The global spread of the U.S. banking industry took place as a result of and to help the spread of other transnational corporations. And it is not hard to see why the expansion was so sudden and so widespread. As Richard Barnet and Ronald Müller reported in their 1974 book *Global Reach:*

> The top 298 U.S. based global corporations studied by the [U.S.] Department of Commerce earn 40% of their entire net profits outside the United States. . . . 122 of the top U.S. based multinational corporations had a higher rate of profits from abroad than from domestic operations. In the office equipment field, for example, the overseas profit for 1971 was 25.6% compared with a domestic profit of 9.2%. The average reported profit of the pharmaceutical industry from foreign operations was 22.4% as against 15.5% from operations in the United States. The food industry reported profits from overseas of 16.7% as compared with U.S. profits of 11.5%.

Huge profits from relatively low investments abroad were not uncommon. The authors pointed out that United Brands, for example, reported a profit of 72.1%; Parker Pen, 51.2%; and Exxon, 52.5%.

Reflecting this profitability, transnational corporations in the United States have been moving their assets abroad at a brisk pace. About a third of the assets of chemical and pharmaceutical industries, about 40% of the consumer goods industry and about 75% of the electrical industry were located outside the United States in 1973. The huge oil industry is estimated to have half its assets abroad. This trend has created pockets of unemployment among American workers and apologists for transnational corporations have made something of a virtue of this, as indicating the truly international spirit of the corporations. All it does indicate, however, is lack of concern for people, for the stock ownership of these large corporations remains concentrated in their parent countries and less than 2% of their high level executives are foreigners. Where transnational corporations have sold shares to the public in host countries, the motive has not been to diversify control but to minimize the company's capital investment. When this happens in a developing country, it soaks up scarce finance capital and weaker and less glamorous local firms suffer. "Incredible as it may seem," note Barnet and Müller, "the poor countries have been an indispensable source of finance capital for the worldwide expansion of global corporations."

To understand the magnitude of the impact these firms have had on the modern world it is necessary to look at their size. Each of the largest four corporations has a sales volume in excess of $10 billion, and more than 200 have passed the $1 billion level. The annual revenues of the largest of them, Exxon, in 1979 was more than the entire GNP of Saudi Arabia. In fact, size is so important a factor that in a 1973 report[4] the United Nations Secretariat noted that "for most practical purposes those with less than $100 million in sales can safely be ignored." The report added that "closely related to their large size is the predominantly oligopolistic character of multinational corporations. Typically, the markets in which they operate are dominated by a few sellers or buyers." The report also said that eight of the ten largest corporations were based in the United States. A third of all foreign affiliates belonged to firms based in the U.S. too. Added to the affiliates of firms in the United Kingdom, the Federal Republic of Germany and France, the number accounted for more than three-quarters of the total.

In addition to their size and global spread, the significance of transnational corporations rests in what they control:

- To a great extent they control the world's finance capital. Despite repeated exhortations at the U.N., the share of official development assistance has been falling steadily and that of bank lending on commercial terms has been rising. Only the recent emergence of the oil-exporting countries as a source of capital has affected the world situation.
- They control the technology necessary for industrialization. A 1964 U.N. study showed, for example, that in India, Pakistan, Trinidad and Tobago, Turkey and the United Arab Republic more than 89% of valid patents were held by foreigners. In many countries it is not merely the patents that are controlled by entire industries. In 1962 Mexico's rubber, electrical machinery and transportation industries were 100% foreign owned. In 1970 some 68% of its metal industry was in foreign hands, as was 100% of the tobacco industry (up from 42% and 17% respectively in 1962). In Brazil in 1970 global corporations took over 60% of the total net profits from the rubber, motor vehicles, machinery, household supplies and mining industries. In 1971 their share was up to 70%.[5]
- They possess information about marketing possibilities and techniques unmatched by any other national or international entity. The growth of transnational advertising agencies in the post-World War II period is indicative of their influence. In 1954 the top U.S. advertising agencies— which dominate the world scene—got about 5% of their total revenues

from other countries. By 1972 not only had this total grown seven-fold to $7 billion, but a full third of it came from overseas. A 1978 U.N. study showed 21 U.S. advertising agencies getting 42% of their total billings overseas. The important thing here, however, is not the inflow of money but the activity it represents. Advertising agencies sell consumption patterns; they are avowed propagandists of giant corporations. Developing countries have been paying for this service, creating among their own people tastes that are not, to say the least, "developmental." And it is not merely a problem of "elites" in developing countries being influenced to imitate Western modes. Advertising can influence poor people as well, and the effects can be disastrous—a case in point being the use of baby food by poor parents who use it in inadequate quantity and with improper hygiene, and end up killing their own children.[6]

Table 4.1 Cultural Commodities Export (in percent).

Commodity	Developed Countries		Developing Countries	
	1971	1974	1971	1974
Paper and Paperboard	98.88	98.12	1.12	1.88
Newsprint Paper	99.34	98.78	0.66	1.22
Coated Printing Paper	99.72	99.57	0.28	0.43
Printing, Binding Machinery	99.54	99.56	0.46	0.44
Printed Matter	94.70	92.85	5.30	7.15
Printed Books	93.40	91.51	6.60	8.49
Television Receivers	94.88	94.78	5.12	5.22
Radio Receivers	87.16	78.22	12.84	21.78
Sound Recorders	98.12	94.70	1.88	5.30
Photo, Cinema Supplies	98.74	98.32	1.26	1.68
Developed Cinema Film	79.55	76.73	20.45	23.27

• They dominate the mass communications field. Four wire service agencies based in the United States, United Kingdom and France provide most of the foreign news that appears in the daily papers of developing countries. These agencies can select—and in fact are forced to do so by exigencies of editorial responsibility—the events that will be publicized. How an event will be presented is also their choice. As most staff members of these agencies are from industrially developed countries the selection process is unavoidably biased in cultural and often in political terms. Two global radio services, the Voice of America and the BBC, add to the bias, as do mass circulation magazines such as *Time, Newsweek* and the *Reader's Digest.* The world view of these services and publications is invariably skewed, judged from the point of view of the developing world, for events in far away Western countries often receive more attention than events in a neighboring country.

• Developed countries are also the main producers of films, television shows, records, books, special interest magazines and other communications material. Most of this material is produced primarily for home markets and then exported to poorer countries. In the case of films and television this can often mean that local production of these items becomes impossible because the producer from the developed country can often offer ridiculously low prices for his products. Not only is the export of these communications commodities profitable, it offers an unparalleled opportunity for developed country perceptions to be presented to a global audience.

In the 1970s there have been several important changes in the pattern of activities of transnational corporations. One is the resurgence of West German and Japanese companies, a counterpoint to the earlier expansion of American firms. The other is the continued growth of the corporate interests as a whole. Their direct investment stock increased in terms of current dollars from $105 billion in 1967 to $158 billion in 1971 and to $287 billion in 1976.[7]

A pronounced feature of this growth has been the expansion of the banking sector. Between 1971 and 1976 the world's largest 50 banks increased their foreign units by 60% to a total of nearly 3,000. The rate of expansion was greatest in developing countries.[8] Foreign assets, loans and earnings have also risen as a result, the figures for developing countries being particularly spectacular (see tables). This development is profoundly significant. Far more than a company digging up ore or producing television sets, a bank is capable of wielding influence in the economies of developing countries. Not only are their networks of interests wider, but their assets are fluid and easily moved. The power they have to retaliate against any developing country trying to nationalize foreign assets is considerable. The situation of many poor countries was unwittingly summed up by the following exchange which appeared in *Barrons*,[9] a publication of the Wall Street firm of Dow Jones:

Komanoff: Charlie, what about the possibility of nationalization?
Maxwell: We've looked at that very carefully, Irv, and we don't think it's much of a threat. Obviously, the market thinks it is, and it's this dichotomy between our perception of the developing situation and the market's backward look at the problems of Indonesian producers that presents the opportunity. Indonesia's faith and credit as a country is held on a slender straw of the continued support of the Western banking system, and we don't think it's really in a position to move against the oil industry.
It's critical for the country's survival. That's a very narrow straw, and the bankers have got their hands on it. In real terms, you could say that Indonesia is already under water and is only breathing through that straw. The other thing, of course, is that the Indonesians already nationalized some years ago, and the work contracts there have been sharply tightened. In our estimates for Natomas, we're using these tightened terms.

Table 4.2 Direct Investment and Other Financial Resource Flows to Developing Countries[a] by Type and Source, 1970 and 1974–1976 (millions of dollars)

Type of flow	1970	1974	1975	1976
A. DAC bilateral				
I. Private flows, total................................	6,401	13,381	19,875	19,089
(a) Direct investment............................	3,543	7,084	10,494	7,593
(b) Bilateral portfolio investment...........	716	3,816	5,239	6,072
(c) Export credits................................	2,142	2,481	4,142	5,424
II. Official flows...	6,535	10,456	12,760	12,687
Total DAC bilateral............................	12,936	23,837	32,635	31,776
B. International bank lending[b]........................	500	8,000	8,500	18,600
C. OPEC bilateral and multilateral.................	400[c]	5,952	8,164	7,955
D. Socialist countries.....................................	890	1,100	840	620
E. Flows from multilateral agencies................	1,784	4,650	6,423	6,743
Total......................................	16,510	43,539	56,562	65,694

Shares of private direct investment (A.I.a) in:	(percentage)			
Total flow...................................	21.4	16.3	18.6	11.6
Total DAC bilateral flow (A)......................	27.4	29.7	32.2	23.9
Total DAC bilateral private flow (A.II)......	55.4	52.9	52.8	39.8

[a]Flows to developing countries as defined by the Development Assistance Committee (DAC), including, in addition to the developing countries in Africa, Asia and the Middle East, and the Western Hemisphere (in accordance with the United Nations classification of countries), eight European countries (Cyprus, Gibraltar, Greece, Malta, Portugal, Spain, Turkey, Yugoslavia). The total recorded net flow of resources to these countries in 1975 amounted to $2.7 billion. Since information on the components of this flow is not available in sufficient detail to adjust the various flows so as to exclude these countries from the present table, the data are not fully comparable with aggregates for "developing countries" shown elsewhere in this report.

[b]Excluding new lending to OPEC countries which is reported by the Bank for International Settlements in its Annual Report for 1976–1977 to have amounted to about $3 billion in 1975 and almost $10 billion in 1976. The data on international bank lending have been adjusted to exclude transactions reported by individual DAC member countries in their statistics on bilateral resource flows.

[c]OECD estimate of average flow in 1970–1972.

Source: United Nations Centre on Transnational Corporations, based on Organisation for Economic Co-operation and Development, *Development Co-operation* (Paris, various years).

Table 4.3 Twenty-five Leading Advertising Agencies, Total and Foreign Billings, 1976

Agency	Country	Total billings (Millions of dollars)	Foreign billings (Percentage of total)
Interpublic Group of Cos.[a]	United States	1,291	55
Dentsu Advertising	Japan	1,189	. . .
J. Walter Thompson Co.	United States	1,039	50
Young and Rubicam	United States	933	39
Leo Burnett Co.	United States	731	31
Ogilvy and Mather	United States	714	49
Ted Bates and Co.	United States	700	50
BBDO International	United States	635	32
SSC and B Inc.[b]	United States	483	69
D'Arcy-MacManus and Masius	United States	481	47
Grey Advertising	United States	473	28
Foote, Cone and Belding	United States	455	31
Doyle Dane Bernbach	United States	430	28
Benton and Bowles	United States	413	31
Compton Advertising	United States	394	68
Hakuhodo Advertising	Japan	390	. . .
Dancer-Fitzgerald-Sample[c]	United States	304	16
Kenyon and Eckhardt	United States	288	57
Norman, Craig and Kummel	United States	251	65
Publicis-Intermarco-Farner	France	246	. . .
Daiko Advertising	Japan	232	. . .
Needham, Harper and Steers[d]	United States	229	22
N W Ayer ABH International[e]	United States	221	5
Wells, Rich, Greene	United States	207	2
Marsteller Inc.	United States	192	24

[a]The group consists of McCann-Erickson Worldwide, Campbell-Ewald Worldwide, Erwin Wasey, Inc. and the Marschalk Company, Inc.

[b]Participant in SSC and B-Lintas International, which had total billings in 1976 of $587 million.

[c]Participant in D-F-S Dorland Fortune, which had total billings in 1976 of $438 million.

[d]Participant in International Needham Univas, which had total billings in 1976 of $594 million.

[e]Participant in Ayer Barker Hegemann International, which had total billings in 1976 of $344 million.

Source: United Nations Centre on Transnational Corporations, based on *Advertising Age,* vol. 48, Nos. 11 and 16 (March 14 and April 18, 1977).

5

The Unions of the Poor

AN UNCERTAIN START

In March 1947, as the British packed to leave India, a conference unlike any
before it or since met in New Delhi. Under a colorful "shamiana" (the
modern version of the court tent of the Moghuls), the Asian Relations
Conference met for ten days. It was a gathering not so much of states as of
states-in-birth. Colonialism was in retreat across Asia and people came from
every corner of the continent to plan a joint future. Unlike the conferences
the Western powers organized to plan the postwar world, the Asian
conference had no strictly defined aims, no strategies plotted beforehand to
achieve calculated ends. Discussions covered a wide area of interaction
among the continent's varied societies: their shared history and cultural
traditions, their common bonds of political and economic interests.

The conference showed just how shaky was the start of the postcolonial
period of world history. India, the host country, was itself not free yet and
was passing through the bloody traumas of partition and civil war. Interim
governments in New Delhi and Karachi were already in position but the
new Pakistani authorities boycotted the meeting because it was an Indian
initiative. A number of West Asian states were absent for they wanted the
conference to take a strong stand against what they considered a new
onslaught of Western imperialism in Palestine, a stand not possible in an
India that was still British-controlled. Egypt, however, sent a full delegation,
as did Iran and Lebanon. Turkey, which considered itself a European state,
sent an observer. So did the Arab League and the Hebrew University in
Palestine. The inevitable confrontation between Arabs and Jews in New
Delhi presaged the acrimonies of battle and the division of Palestine.

If the Far West and south of Asia were in flames, so was the Far East.
China was at civil war and the delegation in New Delhi represented the
losing side. Korea was divided, one-half occupied by the armies of the

Soviet Union, the other by American troops. Japan, too, was occupied, defeated and humiliated (newspapers in New Delhi speculated that Japanese absence from the conference meant either that their invitation had been intercepted by the British or that the Americans had prevented their coming). The Philippines, recently released from American tutelage, chose the period of the conference to sign an agreement with the United States ensuring them a strong military presence in Southeast Asia. In Indonesia and Malaysia colonialism was still very much alive. Malaysia's chief delegate characterized its new constitution as one that "contained the seeds of disunity because its chief supporters were the British planters and mercantile syndicates.", Indonesia's chief delegate reported that the Dutch were continuing their brutal attempts to prolong colonial rule by partitioning Java and encouraging the separation of West Borneo.

On the mainland things were no better. Ho Chi Minh, on his 57th birthday, was appealing to the French to end the costly and fruitless war. "We declare solemnly," he said, "that the Vietnamese people desire only unity and independence within the French Union and we pledge ourselves to respect French economic and cultural interests in Vietnam." The Vietnamese delegate at the conference made a very favorable impression on everyone with his clear and forthright speech, noted Indian delegate and historian Kalidas Nag. But the delegates from Cochin-China, Cambodia and Laos were, in his view, "not very impressive." And as for the Cambodian delegate, Dang Ngoc Chan, he "professed loyalty to the French-protected King of Cambodia . . . but whether they dissociated themselves from the freedom movement in Indo-China was left vague." Siam sent a strong delegation and so did Burma which was shortly to be free.

The conference reflected an Asia unstable, weak and bloodied. Events showed with tragic clarity the power of foreigners to disrupt and control. From China to Palestine countries were threatened with disunion, the result mainly of foreign interference in their political, economic and religious life. Undoubtedly, as Kalidas Nag noted in his account of the Pan-Asian Conference, "after a slumber of ages Asia was awake"; but this was not enough to ensure the implementation of the proposals adopted by the conference for "greater coordination and cooperation among Asian countries." Internal problems and external aggression kept attentions focused on survival in the period that followed. Even a scheduled reconvening of the conference in China in 1949 was not possible.

It was not until 1955 that mutual support crystallized into cooperation. By then a semblance of stability had come to Asia and Africa was beginning its own processes of decolonization. It was the chilliest period of the cold war; the distant guns of Quemoy and Matsu seemed to many the warning shots of a nuclear war. When leaders from 29 African and Asian states met in the cool hill-girt town of Bandung in Indonesia, the possibility of war weighed heavily. "No task is more urgent than of preserving peace,"

President Sukarno told the delegates in his inaugural address. "Without peace our independence means little. The rehabilitation and building of our countries will have little meaning. Our revolutions will not be allowed to run their course." The first task at Bandung, he said, was to "seek an understanding of each other." To facilitate the process, Jawaharlal Nehru of India, the grey eminence at the meeting (he was, with the exception of the 70-year-old Japanese representative, the oldest of the leaders present), suggested that no public debate be held. If differences were aired they would only be used by foreign interests to foment trouble. Several countries supported the proposal; malign outside interest was evident in everything from press commentary to the foreign diplomat whom President Sukarno had quoted in his speech as saying "we will turn this Asian African conference into an afternoon tea meeting."[1] But other countries present— especially those that had thrown in their lot with the Western bloc— Pakistan, Iran and the Philippines, wanted a debate. Much to Prime Minister Nehru's chagrin this was agreed to and the debate that ensued threatened to end Afro-Asian cooperation before it could start. The pro-Western countries proceeded to make strongly anticommunist statements, and the general expectation was that the Chinese, replying in kind, would create a rift that could not be healed. Iraq's Mohammad Fadhil Jamali declared, for instance, "As far as my country is concerned, we feel that there are three international forces in the world today that disturb peace and harmony and that need to be dealt with, with realism and determination." The first was "old style colonialism"; the second was Zionism; and the third was communism—"the one-sided materialistic religion." The communists, he said, "confront the world with a new form of colonialism, much deadlier than the old one. Today the communist world has subject races in Asia and Eastern Europe . . . Turkistan, Estonia, Latvia and Lithuania . . . were swallowed by the Soviet Union . . . also Poland, Romania and Czechoslovakia." He called for "ideological disarmament" and "moral rearmament."

The Philippine delegate, Carlos P. Romulo, made his point more delicately. "The handwriting of history is spread on the wall but not everybody reads it the same way or interprets similarly what he reads there." It is, he continued,

perilously easy in this world for national independence to be more fiction than fact . . . because it expresses the deepest desires of so many people. It can be unscrupulously used as a shibboleth, as a facade, as an instrument for a new and different kind of subjection. I know that on this score there are violently different opinions in the world. I can recall how new nations like India, Indonesia and Ceylon were called puppets of imperialism when they were newly born to freedom. And of course the Philippines republic has been described by these same sources as a mere tool of the United States. . . . On the other hand there is the way some of us view the position of certain other countries which from our own perspective we consider as subservient to other powers. I wonder if in such countries you could read in the press or hear in the public speeches of their spokesmen anything resembling the open criticisms and other attacks that were common fare in places like India and the Philippines even before independence?

Chinese Prime Minister Chou En-lai sat impassively through these speeches, taking notes, cheerful in conversation with other delegates during the breaks in the meeting. Outside, his delegation had charged the United States with trying to sabotage the conference, pointing to the plane crash that killed some members of the Chinese group en route to Bandung and to the announcement in Washington that week of increased aid to Asian allies.[2] But Chou En-lai referred to none of this in his speech; he was the soul of moderation, the voice of pacific reason. "We should seek common ground among ourselves," he said. "Many independent countries have appeared since the Second World War. One group led by the communist parties; another group led by nationalists. . . . Is there any reason why we cannot understand and respect each other? We are all backward economically . . . why could not we ourselves understand each other and enter into friendly cooperation?" Replying to the allegation that China oppressed religious minorities, he pointed to a member of his delegation—"a pious Imam of the Islamic faith." And it was unjust to accuse China of subversive activities, he pointed out, when China itself was the victim of such activities. "As the Chinese proverb says, 'Do not do unto others what you yourself do not desire.' We are against outside interference; how could we want to interfere in the internal affairs of others?" Such heavy oil calmed the waters and the conference went on to adopt a broadly phrased declaration encouraging ideological coexistence. The major beneficiaries of this declaration were countries which had no wish for alliances with the big powers. Bandung set the stage for the nonaligned movement to begin, and during the next few years an increasing number of poor and newly-independent countries would perceive an alternative to the joyless choices of the cold war.

The final declaration at Bandung called for "prior consultation of participating countries in international forums with a view . . . to furthering their mutual economic interests." This became the legislative basis for the Afro-Asian Group at the United Nations, a caucus that previously had met only on an ad hoc basis. After Bandung it met regularly, during the period of swiftest growth in U.N. membership. In 1955, 15 countries joined the United Nations, six of them African and Asian; another 17 joined in 1960, all of them from Africa or Asia. From the status of a minority group unable to defend national or regional interests against the massive bloc of votes commanded by the United States, the Afro-Asian group grew, in the space of a decade, into the dominant influence in the Assembly (see table 5.1).

The manner in which the group operated allowed maximum freedom for national differences. As Dr. Mohammad El Farra, the Jordanian Ambassador to the United Nations put it, "Freedom of action is left to all members. . . . It is very often repeated within the group when divergences of opinion arise on important questions that 'this is not a party meeting to consider party matters. We are not representatives of one party but representatives of sovereign and independent states.' Thus it is not the influence of the group which unites its members but the influence of

Table 5.1 U.N. Membership by Year of Admission.

1945	Argentina, Australia, Belgium, Bolivia, Brazil, Byelorussia SSR, Canada, Chile, China, Colombia, Costa Rica, Cuba, Czechoslovakia, Denmark, Dominican Republic, Ecuador, Egypt, El Salvador, Ethiopia, France, Greece, Guatemala, Haiti, Honduras, India, Iran, Iraq, Lebanon, Liberia, Luxembourg, Mexico, Netherlands, New Zealand, Nicaragua, Norway, Panama, Paraguay, Peru, Philippines, Poland, Saudi Arabia, South Africa, Syria, Turkey, Ukrainian SSR, USSR, United Kingdom, United States of America, Uruguay, Venezuela, Yugoslavia
1946	Afghanistan, Iceland, Sweden, Thailand
1947	Pakistan, Yemen
1948	Burma
1949	Israel
1950	Indonesia
1951	
1952	
1953	
1954	
1955	Albania, Austria, Democratic Kampuchea, Finland, Hungary, Ireland, Italy, Jordan, Laos, Libya, Nepal, Portugal, Romania, Spain, Sri Lanka
1956	Japan, Morocco, Sudan, Tunisia
1957	Ghana, Malaysia
1958	Guinea
1959	
1960	Benin, Central African Empire, Chad, Congo, Cyprus, Gabon, Ivory Coast, Madagascar, Mali, Niger, Nigeria, Senegal, Somalia, Togo, United Republic of Cameroon, Upper Volta, Zaire
1961	Mauritania, Mongolia, Sierra Leone, Tanzania
1962	Algeria, Burundi, Jamaica, Rwanda, Trinidad and Tobago, Uganda
1963	Kenya, Kuwait
1964	Malawi, Malta, Zambia
1965	Bulgaria, Gambia, Maldives, Singapore
1966	Barbados, Botswana, Guyana, Lesotho
1967	Democratic Yemen
1968	Equatorial Guinea, Mauritius, Swaziland
1969	
1970	Fiji
1971	Bahrain, Bhutan, Oman, Qatar, United Arab Emirates
1972	
1973	Bahamas, German Democratic Republic, Federal Republic of Germany
1974	Bangladesh, Grenada, Guinea-Bissau
1975	Cape Verde, Comoros, Mozambique, Papua New Guinea, Sao Tome and Principe, Surinam
1976	Angola, Samoa, Seychelles
1977	Djibouti, Vietnam
1978	Solomon Islands
1979	Dominica, St. Lucia

common interests on important questions which creates the unity of the group."[3] After 1955 the group began to meet frequently, at least once a week during the regular sessions of the General Assembly. The meetings were informal, without records, and open only to group members. They could be convened by the Chairman upon the request of any member state, and the chairmanship rotated alphabetically on a monthly basis. Discussions centered on issues, and votes were seldom taken.

As one observer noted:[4]

> The group clearly functions on the basis of give and take. They realistically believe that each member or grouping of members will sooner or later have before the Assembly one or more issues of major interest to them; since there is always the need to assure enough votes to influence the outcome of the Assembly decisions on these particular issues, the Afro-Asian group members are willing to trade their votes on one issue for the sake of getting the votes of other countries sooner or later on the questions that are particularly important to them.

THE NON-ALIGNED

In the late fifties and early sixties the need for a more activist and coherent approach by the Afro-Asian group become ever more apparent. The cold war had, predictably, been inconclusive, but positions remained frozen and tensions high. In several areas armed intervention by big powers had led to war. The long blood-letting in Vietnam continued. Britain and France, with Israeli cooperation, tried unsuccessfully to "protect" the Suez Canal from Egyptian takeover. The danger of nuclear Armageddon seemed to grow, especially during acute crises between the United States and the Soviet Union, as in Berlin and Cuba. There was an obvious need for measures to relax tensions, and the initiative came from the Afro-Asian Group in the form of the Non-Aligned Movement.

The 25 countries which founded the movement met for the first time in Belgrade, Yugoslavia, in 1961. They met there in order to highlight the fact that the host country was concerned for its independence because of the policies of the Soviet Union in Eastern Europe. In 1956, while the Suez crisis held the world's attention, Soviet military power had curbed the Imre Nagy regime in Hungary; President Tito of Yugoslavia, as part of an effort to reemphasize his own country's independence, became the first host and European member of what is still a predominantly Afro-Asian movement.

After the first summit in 1961 the leaders of the Non-Aligned met in Cairo in 1964, Lusaka in 1970, Algiers in 1973 and Colombo in 1976. With each meeting the membership grew, the original 25 increasing to 47 at Cairo, 53 at Lusaka, 75 at Algiers, 85 at Colombo and 95 at Havana. Today the movement includes almost all African countries, most Asian states and a few from Latin America and Europe. The diversity of the membership is

spectacular, ranging from tiny Gambia with its half-million population, to India; from conservative, religious and oil-rich Saudi Arabia to socialist Cuba dependent on its blockaded sugar exports for survival; from the "least developed" Central African Republic (neé Empire) to Argentina and Yugoslavia which narrowly escape classification as developed countries. The diversity is further widened by the presence as observers of some other developing countries, including most Latin American states, which initially had steered clear of nonalignment. Also present as guests at recent summit conferences were Austria, Finland, the Philippines, Romania, Sweden and Switzerland. At the 1978 ministerial meeting in Belgrade, Pakistan, too, joined the guests and in 1979 it became a full member. Evidently the movement continues to attract new members. And much to the surprise of commentators, every Non-Aligned summit has adopted clear and strong statements of policy despite the range of philosophies among the participants.

The secret of Non-Aligned coherence and activism is not hard to fathom. Small, weak countries do not want to be bullied. By acting as a group, they hope to safeguard their independence. This is why, though the movement was founded in the context of the cold war, its relevance has not decreased in a period much touted for detente. Not only is there the possibility, as Sri Lanka's ex-Prime Minister Sirimavo Bandaranaike noted in her inaugural address at the 1976 Colombo summit, that "detente between the great powers might deteriorate into mutual accommodation and peaceful competition for influence," but, as ex-Prime Minister Indira Gandhi said later, there was the matter of the legacy of the cold war and of colonialism.

Many of our nations remain politically vulnerable to external pressures. The effort to undermine the power of nationalism and political cohesion, to discredit and remove leaders and governments who symbolize independent thinking and self-reliance, and to install more pliable individuals and parties is unabated. Economic exploitation persists in old and new garbs. So do the technological disparities and psychological complexes bred by colonialism. Instead of diminishing, military presences are being extended, and theories of imagined power vacuums are mooted to justify such action.

As stated in the Colombo Declaration,

The bipolar world in which there were only two important centers of power disappeared over a decade ago. Since then attempts to establish a multipolar world have proved futile as the majority in the international community are against polarisation around power centers. The majority also reject the notions of international order based on power blocs, balance of power and spheres of influence, as all such notions are inconsistent with aspirations towards the true independence of states and democratisation of international relations.

It is not difficult to see how countries as different as Saudi Arabia and Cuba can subscribe to this analysis. Nor is it difficult to understand the attraction of nonalignment for small states of every continent, even those supposedly secure in warm alliances with big powers.

Over the years there have been several attempts to give firmer structural forms to the nonaligned movement but these have been resisted by the majority, including the most influential among them. Again, the reasons are not esoteric. In large measure the vitality and efficacy of the movement are based on its flexible means of operation. Policies are set at meetings of the entire membership at the highest level, once every three years. These summits are preceded by a meeting the year before of foreign ministers of all members and followed the year after by a ministerial-level meeting of the Coordinating Bureau. A variety of ad hoc and standing committees keep tabs on matters of special interest, while overall coordination rests for three-year periods with the host countries of the summit meetings. The closest thing to a structure the Non-Aligned countries have is a Coordinating Bureau at U.N. Headquarters in New York. "The Bureau here provides the ongoing mechanism for the movement," says Salman Haidar, India's Deputy Permanent Representative at the U.N. "It serves as a clearing house for ideas, the place where people first bring new initiatives. It meets as and when required. On a daily basis during the annual sessions of the General Assembly." Even these loose arrangements are not permanently mandated: each summit decides on what is to be done and on how best to do it.

In the early years the Non-Aligned focused upon the major political problems of decolonization, racism, and the cold war. By the beginning of the 1970s, however, the focus had begun to shift. As Tanzanian President Julius Nyerere told a preparatory meeting for the 1970 summit, "It is no longer enough to meet and complain to each other and to the world about international bullying. Everyone now knows that this bullying goes on. And we have already declared our intention of standing up to such behaviour." The Non-Aligned were militarily weak, he said, and to talk of defending themselves by joint force of arms was sheer fantasy. "The real and urgent threat to the independence of almost all the Non-Aligned states comes not from the military but from the economic power of the big states. It is poverty which constitutes our greatest danger."

In attempting to overcome poverty the countries of Africa, Asia and Latin America were forced to enter into unfair and injurious relationships with the industrialized countries. It was time, Mr. Nyerere said, for Non-Aligned nations to cooperate on the economic front. Unlike other forms of cooperation among the members of the movement, this need not be merely a pooling of weaknesses; it could be the source of considerable strength.

THE GROUP OF 77

President Nyerere was not alone in thinking as he did. During the next few years, and particularly at the 1973 Algiers summit, the Non-Aligned focused increasingly on economic matters. In doing so they reflected the development of another movement of developing countries—that of the Group of 77. In many ways the two groups have had a symbiotic relationship, their initiatives reinforcing and often being indistinguishable from one another. The difference is in the size of the membership—the "77" includes all the developing countries in the United Nations (119 in 1979). Unlike the Non-Aligned Movement, however, it includes countries militarily allied to the great powers as well as all the Latin American states. To understand why, it is necessary to look to the beginning of the first United Nations Development Decade.

In 1961, as the decade got off to its hopeful start, the General Assembly decided unanimously that international trade was the "primary instrument for economic development" and that a world conference might be necessary to set policy. The Secretary-General was asked [Resolution 1717 (XVI)] to consult governments on the matter. The result was a decision the next year to convene a U.N. Conference on Trade and Development (UNCTAD). A 32-member committee of experts was set up to prepare the agenda and documentation. It was during this phase that the Latin American countries began to understand the importance of a united front with the Africans and Asians. After the conference in Geneva, in 1964, they issued a joint declaration stating that,

> The developing countries regard their unity as the outstanding feature of this conference. This unity has sprung out of the fact that facing the basic problems of development they have a common interest in a new policy for international trade and development. . . . Their solidarity has been tested in the course of the conference and they have emerged from it with even greater unity and strength.

The unity of the group, the Declaration continued,

> is an indispensable instrument for securing the adoption of new attitudes and new approaches in the international economic field. This unity is also an instrument for enlarging the area of cooperative endeavor in the international field and for securing mutually beneficient relationships with the rest of the world. Finally, it is a necessary means for cooperation amongst the developing countries themselves.

The members of the group pledged themselves "to maintain, foster and strengthen this unity." To this end they undertook to "adopt all possible means to increase the contacts and consultations among themselves." The 77 countries which signed the declaration gave the new group its name.

The developing countries at the UNCTAD conference succeeded in getting agreement on the creation of new international machinery in the field of trade and development. They did not get, as they had hoped, a comprehensive International Trade Organization (ITO), but they did get a permanent organ of the General Assembly which would act:

(a) To promote international trade, especially with a view to accelerating economic development, particularly trade between countries at different stages of development, between developing countries and between countries with different systems of economic and social organization, taking into account the functions performed by existing international organizations;

(b) To formulate principles and policies on international trade and related problems of economic development;

(c) To make proposals for putting the said principles and policies into effect and to take such other steps within its competence as may be relevant to this and having regard to differences in economic systems and stages of development;

(d) Generally, to review and facilitate the coordination of activities of other institutions within the United Nations system in the field of international trade and related problems of economic development, and in this regard to cooperate with the General Assembly and the Economic and Social Council with respect to the performance of their responsibilities for coordination under the Charter of the United Nations;

(e) To initiate action, where appropriate, in cooperation with the competent organs of the United Nations for the negotiation and adoption of multilateral legal instruments in the field of trade, with due regard to the adequacy of existing organs of negotiation and without duplication of their activities;

(f) To be available as a centre for harmonizing the trade and related development policies of government and regional economic groupings in pursuance of Article 1 of the Charter;

(g) To deal with any other matters within the scope of its competence.[5]

The new UNCTAD secretariat had only a limited budget and little capacity for operational measures, but it would be prolific in the number of studies it conducted, exploring the problems of developing countries from their viewpoints. The changes in structure, practice and principle necessary in global systems dominated by a few rich countries became apparent in the process. As a result not only was there a new perception of economic problems, but the unity of the 77 was strengthened in demanding change. In recognition of UNCTAD's role, the Group of 77 decided, at a 1967 meeting in Algiers that they "should meet at the ministerial level as often as this may be deemed necessary, and in any case always prior to the convening of sessions of the U.N. Conference on Trade and Development."

The working methods of the 77 are, like those of the Non-Aligned, loose, flexible and very much dependent on the activism of the coordinating members. Initially these coordinating countries, "the Group of 27" were nominated, but now all interested countries involve themselves in the process. As with the Non-Aligned, the focal point of coordination is New York, though with UNCTAD headquartered in Geneva much of the action takes place there.

6

The Stirring Seventies

As the Non-Aligned Movement and the Group of 77 began to work in tandem, the effects were evident not only at world conferences but in national economic policies. Even countries considered firm allies of the major industrialized states began to demand changes in the nature of their foreign economic relations. The most significant of these demands came from a group of countries which had, in 1960, formed the Organization of Petroleum Exporting Countries (OPEC). Founded by Iran, Iraq, Kuwait, Saudi Arabia and Venezuela to keep the price of oil from dropping, OPEC tried throughout the sixties and early seventies for changes in the systems of production and pricing imposed by an international cartel of giant oil companies. By 1970 OPEC had grown to 10 members with the addition of Abu Dhabi, Algeria, Indonesia, Libya and Qatar; Nigeria and Ecuador joined four years later. Together, they accounted for nearly 50% of world oil production and nearly 90% of world oil exports. Yet until the 1970s, they were virtually powerless to benefit from this situation.

In negotiating with the oil companies, the West Asian countries had learned from experience to tread warily. Iran, for instance, had nationalized its British-owned oil industry in the fifties, only to face a ruinous boycott organized by the powerful cartel. Prime Minister Mohammad Mossadegh, whose government was responsible for nationalization, was overthrown; he spent the rest of his life in prison.

But the world situation was different in 1971 when the Shah of Iran led the OPEC team in negotiations with the oil companies. Though he had been returned to power in Iran by the action of the oil companies against Mossadegh, the Shah's attitude in the 1971 Teheran talks showed little that could be interpreted as gratitude. He warned the oil companies in public that they would "precipitate a dangerous crisis if they formed a cartel to try to intimidate OPEC's membership into abandoning their legitimate claims." The crisis, he said, would be "even more dangerous if the Western governments try to back up and protect the companies." Such action would open the way to a confrontation between the "economic imperialist powers" on the one hand and the developing countries on the other. "Then anything could happen, not only a stoppage of the oil, but a much more terrible rebellion of the have-nots against the haves."[1]

In the face of this threat the oil companies gave ground. Over the following months they continued to offer concessions as OPEC gained in confidence. Assessing the events of 1971 the OPEC secretariat in its annual report noted that the group had emerged as a "powerful, internationally recognized oil policy instrument capable of playing an effective role in the international oil industry."[2] *Le Monde*, the Paris based newspaper, asserted that the negotiations had "done more to shake up the question of the development of the nonindustrialized countries than 20 years of verbiage in international organizations and tons of social and economic reports."[3] More shaking up was in store. A month after the fourth Non-Aligned summit in Algiers called for strong cooperative action by developing countries to advance their economic cause, the West Asian members of OPEC initiated a process which stunned the world. They decided to raise the price of oil, first to $3.65 and then to $11.65 a barrel.[4]

Meeting in Kuwait on October 17 the Arab oil ministers also decided to use their control of oil production to exert pressure on countries supporting Israel. "Unless the world corrects the situation by forcing Israel to withdraw from our occupied territories and by making the United States realize the high price for its support, European industrialized countries will pay as a result," said the Declaration they issued. It was decided "to start immediately reducing oil production by not less than 5% per month," creating a worldwide oil shortage. For the first time the shoe was on the other foot. Poor countries were jointly exerting economic pressure for political ends.

The main result of the new terms imposed by OPEC was a massive diversion of funds from the oil companies to the producing countries. Within a few years the much bemoaned "gap" separating the OPEC countries from the industrialized rich had begun to close (see table 6.1).

Table 6.1 Relative Income Gaps: Developing Country Per Capita Incomes as a Percentage of Developed Country Incomes

	1950	1960	1975
Developing Countries:			
Poorest	8.1%	4.0%	2.6%
Middle-Income	20.8	18.3	17.0
Oil-Exporting	n.a.	16.1	22.6
All Developing Countries	11.9	9.7	9.2

Source: World Bank

The psychological impact of all this was electrifying. The industrialized world was shaken; the developing countries exhilarated. There was no doubt that oil-importing developing countries were seriously affected by the rise in oil prices; there was equally little doubt that they applauded the OPEC action and saw in its success their own hope for the future. The mood of the time was captured at the 1974 special session of the U.N. General Assembly convened to discuss "Raw Materials and Development." Requested on short notice by Algeria, the host of the previous Non-Aligned summit, the special session issued a declaration calling for the "Establishment of a New International Economic Order." It was the first time the developing countries within the U.N. got from rich countries a consensus on plans for a comprehensive reshaping of the world order. Although the plan was not detailed, although the consensus hid much acrimony and the richest countries had strong reservations, the resolution marked a watershed in U.N. history.

The next year, in accordance with a resolution of the Algiers Non-Aligned summit, a "Conference of Developing Countries on Raw Materials" was convened in Dakar, Sengal. According to the Dakar Declaration, the conference "carried out a detailed analysis of the fundamental problems of raw materials and development in the light of recent trends in international economic relations" and found the results unsatisfactory. There was a "perpetuation of inequalities in economic relations, imperalist domination, neo-colonialist exploitation and a total lack of solutions to the basic problems of the developing countries." It cannot be denied, the declaration continued, "that the structure and organization of world import and export trade operate for the most part to the advantage of developed countries." The opinion of developed countries that "the free working of the primary products market should normally ensure an optimum distribution of the world's resources" was not realistic, especially in view of the many obstacles that prevented developing countries from getting access to their rich markets. "The framework and organization of commodity trade, and especially the marketing and distribution systems for individual commodities prevailing at present were developed in the 19th century by colonial powers and are wholly inadequate today as instruments of economic change and advancement."

The Dakar Declaration pointed out that "transnational corporations control the production of and trade in many primary commodities, particularly through the exercise of bargaining power against a large number of weak competing sellers in developing countries." World commodity markets experienced a chronic instability because of "sudden and substantial shifts in the balance of world supply and demand, as well as through excessive speculative activities encouraged by the lack of adequate regulation of these markets." The Declaration averred that denying developing countries an adequate role in setting world prices for their commodity exports had "led to a permanent transfer of real resources from developing to developed countries." The benefits from improved productivity of raw materials and commodities in developing countries, instead of bringing them higher earnings, were transferred to the developed consumer countries. This was "in marked contrast to what occurs in developed countries where improvements in productivity result in higher profits for these countries."

Whichever aspect of the world raw material situation the conference considered, it found the status quo dismal. Commodity prices, historically low and unstable, seemed to be heading further downward after a short rising period. Developed countries spend much more on subsidizing domestic production of primary commodities which competed with the products of developing countries, than they did for foreign aid for development. They had not met their obligations under the strategy for the second U.N. Development Decade to readjust their economies to help growth in developing countries. On the contrary their policies of supporting production of commodities competing with the output of poorer countries and dumping surpluses on world markets led to even more depressed prices. "At the same time research and development efforts were undertaken, in particular by transnational corporations . . . and led to the large-scale production of synthetics and substitutes which displaced in well protected markets the natural products exported by developing countries."

Looking further afield, the conference pointed out that "the fast growth of developed countries was partly financed through an international monetary system tailored to their needs, allowing inflationary trends to affect not only their domestic economies but also international trade." Developing countries, being the weakest partners in this trade, were those who suffered most from inflation. Also, "monetary activities by transnational corporations contributed significantly to the destabilization of the international monetary system." And the devaluation of several developed country currencies in the early seventies had adversely affected the currency reserves held by poorer countries. All this had led to a persistent long-term deterioration in the terms of trade of developing countries (i.e., the prices of their imports constantly escalated in comparison to their exports).

The fundamental problem remained the same. As the conference declaration noted, "Developing countries depend on their commodity exports for 75 to 80% of their foreign exchange earnings. The process of their development is still largely dependent upon external factors, i.e., the demand from the developed countries for their export commodities." The prevailing economic order, "and the international division of labour on which it depends have been based essentially on the exploitation and processing by industrialized countries of the raw materials produced by developing countries. . . . To this must be added the further profits accruing from the processes of marketing, financing, freight and insurance." The only solution was to change the global division of labor so that developing countries increased their capacities to process their own raw materials into manufactured goods.

But such changes obviously would not occur if poorer countries continued their traditional approach to negotiations, which, said the declaration, consisted of "presentation of a list of requests to the developed countries and an appeal to their political goodwill." The conference urged developing countries to "undertake common action to strengthen their bargaining position." The means of achieving economic emancipation was to "recover and control their natural resources and wealth and the means of economic development."

There were few illusions about the difficulty this would involve. The memory of Chilean President Salvador Allende's fate was fresh. Many of the representatives there had listened to Allende's dramatic and desperate appeal for help at the Non-Aligned summit at Algiers. They had seen his attempt to nationalize Chile's rich copper mines result in an economic siege imposed by giant corporations like ITT and Anaconda. They had seen Chile's economy ruined, its democratic system subverted and Allende himself murdered, with the active encouragement and help of the corporations and the U.S. Central Intelligence Agency (CIA).

Despite such dangers—and every meeting of developing countries mentions them—the processes toward economic independence have continued. Both the Group of 77 and the Non-Aligned Movement have adopted blueprints for economic cooperation among developing countries. UNCTAD has created a new committee on the subject. Regional bodies like the Organization for African Unity (OAU) and the Latin American Economic System (SELA) are initiating a variety of joint actions. A number of subregional and sectoral programs for cooperation are underway. But nowhere is cooperative action very advanced. The Group of 77 still feels it necessary to ask, as they did at their ministerial meeting in Manila in 1976, that:

> The developed countries, both the developed market economy countries and the socialist countries of Eastern Europe, should commit themselves to abstain from adopting any kind of measures or action which might undermine the decisions of developing countries in favour of the strengthening of their economic cooperation and the diversification of their production structures.

That this request has gone unheeded is evident from the declaration issued by the Ministerial Meeting of the Non-Aligned in Belgrade in 1978. The ministers pointed "with concern to the more and more overt recourse to interference in the internal affairs of independent, particularly non-aligned, countries in order to influence their socio-political development, their foreign policies, and to circumscribe their independence." Foreign interference is carried out "by means of state power and through other national and international political and economic and financial organizations and institutions, of an official or private nature especially the transnational corporations and mass media used in a global scale," the declaration said. "The modes of foreign interference include direct and indirect aggressive actions, pressures, subversion and organized vilification campaigns, directed especially toward undermining the independent development of the Non-Aligned countries and destablizing their governments, to which end recourse is also made to armed interventions by special forces and mercenaries." Such interference was becoming "one of the principal forms of attack against the Non-Aligned Movement and the unity of the non-aligned countries."

The job of cooperation taken up by the first faltering Pan-Asian Conference moves forward more surely a generation later, but still at a painfully slow pace. It is a sad commentary on the state of the world that despite all the fine words and declarations about the common interests of humanity, international cooperation for development should find its way so crowded with deliberately created obstacles. Such difficulties are almost always ignored in discussing development but, as the two quotations above show, in the considered view of the ministers of more than two-thirds of the world's countries, they are both relevant and important.

7

Work in Progress

The success of OPEC's action in raising oil prices inaugurated a new phase in cooperation among developing countries. This was not merely because of the massive transfer of resources into one part of the developing world—a number of other developments conspired to the same end. One was the emergence of several developing countries with advanced industrial, scientific and technological capabilities. Another was the increasing contradictions within the systems of cooperation created after the Second World War. The rise of Europe and Japan as economic powers competitive with the United States led to the collapse of the world monetary system based on the predominance of the dollar and to strains in trading relationships. The steady growth of the economic power of the socialist group of states, accounting for a third of world production, further modified the workings of the global economy. Early in the 1970s the concern that economic growth would be limited by environmental and resource constraints was acute, and was reflected most sensationally in the Club of Rome's report on the "Limits to Growth." Suddenly all the verities on which postwar economic growth in the world's market economies were based were called in question. The time was ripe for new approaches and arrangements. Thus when OPEC gained control not only of oil but of vast wealth and influence, there was a rush of efforts to reach a variety of bilateral and multilateral agreements among developing countries in trade, investment and production. This burst of activity was not altogether new but it was essentially an acceleration of trends that had existed before OPEC came into the money. Now, as the current decade draws toward its close, it is useful to ask how much progress has been made in the seventies—What is the state of those "bridges across the south"?

TRADE

Throughout the sixties trade among developing countries declined as a share of their total trade. This trend was checked in 1970 and since then has been reversed dramatically. By 1975 the ground lost in the entire previous decade has been regained and one-quarter of all imports and one-fifth of all exports of developing countries were the products of other developing countries.

Table 7.1 Developing Countries: Percentage Share of Mutual Trade and Trade with Developed Market Economies and Centrally Planned Economies in Total Trade[a] 1960–1961, 1969–1970 and 1974–1975

Years	Mutual trade		Trade with developed market economies		Trade with centrally planned economies	
	Exports	Imports[b]	Exports	Imports[b]	Exports	Imports
1960–1961	22.1	20.5	72.8	73.8	4.9	5.7
1969–1970	19.9	19.0	73.5	72.0	5.5	9.0
1974–1975	22.1	25.5	72.8	67.8	4.1	6.7

[a]Based on current dollar value of exports or imports. See also table 7.2, footnote a.
[b]See table 7.2, footnote c.
Source: U.N. Department of International Economic and Social Affairs; document E/AC.54/L.94.

In the first half of the seventies the value of trade among developing countries grew at the phenomenal rate of 35.5 percent (as against 32.7 percent for exports to developed capitalist countries and 25.3 percent for exports to the socialist countries of Eastern Europe and the USSR). If we consider the quantity of trade (rather than the value, which reflects inflation) the figures are even more dramatic. The exports of developing countries to their peers increased at about double the rate of their exports to developed countries: 8.8 percent and 4.5 percent being the respective rates of growth (table 7.2). The nature of their trade and its geographical patterns have also been changing significantly in recent years. At the beginning of the sixties the share of manufactured goods in the nonfuel trade of developing countries stood at about 20 percent. By 1970 this had more than doubled to 44.7 percent. In the following five years it expanded to 51.9 percent of their mutual nonfuel trade.

Among manufactures, the shares of chemicals, machinery and transport equipment have increased more than two-and-a-half times since 1960. Food, beverages and tobacco have shown the sharpest reduction in their share of interdeveloping country trade. In analyzing these trends a 1977 U.N. report[1] pointed out that the most rapid growth seemed to have occurred "precisely in those product groups that have, by and large, been least subject to tariff

Table 7.2 Developing Countries: Average Annual Rate of Increase in
Mutual Trade and in Trade with the Rest of the World,[a]
1960–1961 to 1974–1975 (percentage)

Item and time period	Mutual trade[b]	Trade with developed market economies		Trade with centrally planned economies	
		Exports	Imports	Exports	Imports
Value [c]					
1960–1961 to 1969–1970	6.0	7.5	6.7	8.7	12.4
1969–1970 to 1974–1975	35.5	32.7	26.1	25.3	20.5
Quantum					
1960–1961 to 1969–1970	5.7	6.8	6.4	—	—
1969–1970 to 1974–1975	8.8	4.5	9.6	—	—
Unit price					
1960–1961 to 1969–1970	0.3	0.7	0.5	—	—
1969–1970 to 1974–1975	24.5	27.0	15.1	—	—

[a]Based on merchandise trade valued f.o.b., where the destination is known; for exports this came to some 99 percent of total *recorded* developing country exports. Data for developing countries refer to countries and territories in Latin America and the Caribbean, in Africa other than the Republic of South Africa, in Asia other than Israel, Japan and all those listed as centrally planned (see below) and in Oceania other than Australia and New Zealand; for developed market economies to North America, Western Europe, and Australia, Israel, Japan, New Zealand, Republic of South Africa and Yugoslavia; for centrally planned economies to Eastern Europe and the Union of Soviet Socialist Republics, and China, Democratic People's Republic of Korea, former Democratic Republic of Viet Nam and Mongolia.

[b]Merchandise exports with both origin and reported destination in developing countries.
[c]Based on export data of trade partners and valued f.o.b.

Source: Centre for Development Planning, Projections and Policies of the Department of Economic and Social Affairs of the United Nations Secretariat, based on *Handbook of International Trade and Development Statistics 1976* (United Nations publication, Sales No. E/F.76.II.D.3), United Nations *Yearbook of International Trade Statistics* and *Monthly Bulletin of Statistics* (various issues).

or other forms of protection—such as chemicals or machinery—or where protectionism receded towards the end of the 1960s in several major countries as part of their efforts to raise the over-all level of their industrial efficiency." The report also noted that many of the products successfully traded by developing countries had displaced goods traditionally imported from developed countries. But in some cases "the products originated from

Table 7.3 Developing Countries: Changing Pattern of Intraregional and Interregional Trade, 1960–1961 to 1974–1975

Exporting region[a] and time period	Average Annual Percentage Rate of Increase of Merchandise Exports to:				Percentage Share of Merchandise Exports at the End of Each Period			
	Developing countries			Rest of the world[b]		Developing countries		Rest of the world[b]
	All	Own region	Other developing regions		All	Own region	Other developing regions	
Latin America and Caribbean [c]								
1960–1961 to 1969–1970	6.6	6.7	4.5	5.3	19.9	18.1	1.8	80.1
1969–1970 to 1974–1975	28.8	26.5	46.3	24.2	24.0	19.9	4.1	76.0
South and East Asia [d]								
1960–1961 to 1969–1970	5.1	4.5	6.8	6.8	29.8	22.7	7.1	70.2
1969–1970 to 1974–1975	27.3	24.8	35.3	28.2	29.0	19.8	9.2	71.0
West Asia								
1960–1961 to 1969–1970	7.5	8.6	6.5	9.4	18.6	7.7	10.9	81.4
1969–1970 to 1974–1975	58.0	38.5	68.2	53.4	21.9	4.6	17.3	78.1

Table 7.3 (Cont.) Developing Countries: Changing Pattern of Intraregional and Interregional Trade, 1960–1961 to 1974–1975

Exporting region[a] and time period	Average Annual Percentage Rate of Increase of Merchandise Exports to:				Percentage Share of Merchandise Exports at the End of Each Period			
	Developing countries			Rest of the world[b]	Developing countries			Rest of the world[b]
	All	Own region	Other developing regions		All	Own region	Other developing regions	
Africa [e]								
1960–1961 to 1969–1970	6.0	6.1	5.8	9.0	9.8	5.2	4.6	90.2
1969–1970 to 1974–1975	28.3	19.8	35.8	25.5	11.0	4.1	6.9	89.0

[a]Regions are listed in descending order of relative importance of intraregional trade in 1974–1975.
[b]Including small residual of exports not classified by regional destination.
[c]Based on data which in 1960–1961 included exports of some developing islands in the Pacific.
[d]Including entrepot trade of Singapore. An estimate of intraregional trade excluding such entrepot trade yields the following figures for the share of intraregional trade: 1969–1970, 20.6 percent; 1974–1975, 18.3 percent.
[e]Based on data which in 1960–1961 included exports of Southern Rhodesia, but excluded such exports thereafter.

Source: See table 7.2.

the new subsidiaries in developing countries of the enterprises of developed countries." The extent to which transnational corporations are involved in the trade among developing countries and the implications of this remain to be fully analyzed.

The major change in the geographical distribution of mutual trade among developing countries has been the rapid growth of exchanges between regions. In the sixties only South and East Asia increased their trade with other regions at a faster pace than trade within their own regions. This trend changed during the first half of the seventies. Latin America and the Caribbean, West Asia and Africa all increased their interregional trade at rates substantially higher than the rate of growth in their regional trade. The average annual rate of increase in the intraregional trade of Latin America and the Caribbean was 46.3 percent in the first half of the current decade. For South and East Asia during the same period the figure was 35.3 percent, for West Asia it was 68.2 percent, and for Africa it was 35.8 percent. These figures indicate a trend; they do not as yet signify massive movements of goods from one region to another. For perspective it would be useful to keep in mind that intraregional trade constitutes only 4.1 percent of the Latin American and Caribbean region's total trade; 9.2 percent of that of South and East Asia; 17.3 percent of West Asia; and 6.9 percent of Africa (table 7.3).

Another point to keep in mind is that trade among different regions was pioneered by a very few countries. Between Latin America and Africa the rapid growth of trade is accounted for by Argentinian and Brazilian exchanges with Algeria, Morocco, Zaire and Zambia, and by the Nigerian trade with the Caribbean. Argentina and Brazil are also largely responsible for the increase in their region's trade with West Asia, because of their exports to Iran, Iraq and Syria. South and East Asian exchanges with West Asia involve more countries, but India, Pakistan, Iran, Saudi Arabia and Egypt play key roles.

The establishment of commercial links among the regions can be expected to grow in view of the arrangements being made to encourage the trend. The pioneering effort in this direction was made by Egypt, India and Yugoslavia through a 1968 Tripartite Agreement on trade. This was followed by a 1971 decision within the framework of GATT, clearing the way for preferential tariff reductions to promote trade among developing countries. Consequently a protocol was negotiated by 16 countries[2] granting each other preferential trade concessions in 1973. Some 500 items are covered by the protocol, relating mainly to manufactured and semi-manufactured goods. At the inception of the 1973 agreement, trade in these items amounted to about $40 million; by 1975 the figure had more than doubled to about $100 million. The volume of trade is still small and the number of participating countries relatively few, but the agreement and protocol do point the way for future development.

Other trade promotion efforts have been mainly at the regional and subregional levels, and most have been in the context of regional integration arrangements. One such arrangement is the Bangkok Agreement reached in 1975 by Bangladesh, India, the Lao People's Republic, the Philippines, the Republic of Korea, Sri Lanka and Thailand. Lists of tariff concessions are set out for some 160 items, the trade in which amounted to roughly $50 million in 1975. Tariffs are lowered on the average about a third on agricultural, semiprocessed and manufactured goods. Other provisions of the Agreement cover mutual trade expansion, including commitments not to impose new restrictions on products of export potential and to give special concessions for products produced by joint ventures of participating countries. As yet the Bangkok Agreement is too recent for any judgment as to its efficacy in operation. Nor is experience with other such efforts of much use in estimating its chances of success because other regional efforts at cooperation are too various in nature, scope and aim.

Trade among developing countries is the most visible aspect of mutual cooperation, and the one most often discussed. But there are other areas where cooperation has been attempted or is possible; and of these, little is widely known.

SHARING PEOPLE

During the last two decades a number of developing countries have significantly increased their stock of skilled manpower and their capacity to teach such skills. A 1978 UNCTAD report[3] calls the increase "a veritable explosion," pointing out that "the number of students at the third or higher level of learning in all the developing countries in 1950 was only 930,000 or a bare 10 percent of the world total. By 1972 the figure had increased more than eightfold—to 7,600,000—and the share in the world total had risen to 25 percent. By 1980 this share is expected to rise to nearly 30 percent."

This skilled workforce has been shared with other developing countries, especially the newly affluent members of OPEC. Data about this are poor, but UNCTAD studies show, for instance, that in West Asia immigrant doctors accounted for about 65 percent of the total and that 71 percent of these were from other developing countries. In the case of Africa 85 percent of doctors were foreigners, nearly half of them from other developing countries. UNCTAD studies also show the significance of the trend in skill exporting countries. Between 1971 and 1974, of the Sri Lankan doctors who sought employment abroad, 91 percent traveled to other developing countries; so did 73 percent of accountants and 60 percent of university teachers and lawyers. In the case of Pakistani nationals employed abroad, more than 45 percent were in other developing countries by 1977, and more than 60 percent of all the money they sent home came from OPEC countries.

Table 7.4 Educational Expansion in the Developing Countries,
1950, 1960, 1972

Item	No. in million			Growth 1950–1972		Percentage share	
	1950	1960	1972	Index	% per yr.	1950	1972
Developing countries [a]							
III level	0.93	2.1	7.6	820	10.0	15	25
II level	7.5	18.2	60.5	805	9.9	20	44
I level	64.7	119.0	216.1	334	5.6	37	62
Total	73.2	139.3	284.2	398	6.5	33	55
Developed countries [b]							
III level	5.4	9.1	22.8	423	6.8	85	75
II level	30.5	50.7	76.0	249	4.2	80	56
I level	112.4	124.5	134.7	119	0.8	63	38
Total	148.3	184.3	233.5	158	2.1	67	45
World [a]							
I level	6.3	11.2	30.4	482	7.4	100	100
II level	38.0	68.9	136.5	359	6.0	100	100
III level	177.1	243.5	350.8	206	3.3	100	100
Total	221.5	323.6	517.7	264	4.5	100	100

[a]Excluding China, the Democratic People's Republic of Korea and Viet Nam.
[b]Including North America, Western, Eastern and Southern Europe, USSR, Japan, Australia and New Zealand.

Note: The standardization of international statistics on education has a relatively recent origin. There are therefore some arbitrary choices to be made regarding the classification of different types of schools. Broadly speaking, *I level* corresponds to primary, *II level* to secondary and *III level* to higher education. All data for enrollment in pre-primary education is omitted. Higher primary, intermediate or middle schools and most of the vocational and teacher training schools (unless completion of secondary school was a condition for entry) are included under II level. For definitions, see UNESCO, *Statistical Yearbook*, 1964, p. 77.

There were over half a million foreign students in 50 countries for which information is available. There is thus some double-counting involved in separating figures for developing and developed countries, which would tend to underestimate the number of students from developing countries in the III level, whether enrolled in their own countries or in foreign countries.

Sources: UNESCO, *Statistical Yearbook*, 1972; United Nations, *Statistical Yearbook*, 1975.

TRAINING FACILITIES

In addition to the growing exchange of teachers and students among national schools and universities in developing countries, in recent years there has been an increase in regionally oriented training centers. They range from basic Literacy Centers to institutions training people at the most advanced levels. These facilities are too numerous to list here, but a few are mentioned below to illustrate their wide range:

- Maritime training centers in Brazil and Egypt. Coordination of teaching methods and standardized certification by a number of Asian maritime institutions.
- Social science research and documentation centers in Zaire, Egypt, and Latin America.
- Mass communications institutions with regionally oriented workshops in India, the Philippines and Nigeria.
- Insurance education institutes in the Philippines and Cameroon.
- Regional centers for training in the preservation of cultural and natural heritage in Iraq, Mexico and Nigeria.
- Institutes for manpower planning and administration in Uruguay, Cameroon and Peru.
- An Asian regional center for technology in India and another planned for Africa.

SERVICES

The first comprehensive effort to collect and distribute information about the services developing countries can share with one another was made during the preparations for the TCDC conference. It resulted in the Directory of Services for Technical Co-operation among Developing Countries, covering some 900 organizations in 67 countries. (See also chapter 9, p. 71.) Published by UNDP, the directory lists national and regional organizations in developing countries prepared to offer their services to other developing countries. It covers educational and training institutions, research facilities and technological development institutions, expert and consultancy services. It also provides information sources for classified listings of development services. Entries are in English, French or Spanish, depending upon the international working language of the organization offering the services. Types of services available are listed together with other relevant data.

The directory is supplemented by an index linking economic sectors to organizations in the countries listed. Sixteen sectors, broken down into 88 subsectors, are included: agriculture, forestry and fisheries; cultural and social and human sciences; education; general economic and social policy, planning and public administration; health; industry; international trade and tourism; labor, management and employment; natural resources; population; relief activities; science and technology; social security and other social services; transport and communications; human settlements; environment.

The directory is to be periodically updated as part of a computerized Information Referral System (INRES), which UNDP has set up to collect and disseminate information on the TCDC capacities of developing countries. It will be supplemented by an enquiry service to answer specific requests for information on TCDC services.

SHARING NEWS

To correct the grossly biased and imbalanced flow of world news there have been several attempts by developing countries to create systems of sharing news among themselves. Among the more significant efforts have been the growth of regional cooperation among news agencies in developing countries. In 1975 the Non-Aligned countries organized a pool which now includes more than 40 news agencies and exchanges material through 13 redistribution centers. A similar operation is Inter Press Service (IPS), a journalists' cooperative founded in 1964. Originally it covered only Latin America, but now, with headquarters in Rome, its members work in Africa, Asia, Europe and North America as well. In 1975, 13 English-speaking Caribbean countries set up the Caribbean News Agency (CANA) with the help of UNDP, UNESCO and Reuters. It became an independent news agency the next year, including in its cooperative effort 17 public and private agencies. Similar efforts at cooperation are underway in Africa and Asia.

ECONOMIC INTEGRATION

Many developing countries have small populations. More than half of Africa's independent states, for example, have less than 5 million people. Even where populations are larger, neighboring countries often have shared resources or problems. Because of this there is often a pressing need for countries to integrate their economies and coordinate plans for development at the regional or subregional levels. UNCTAD estimates that as many as 70 countries or territories are already participating in such schemes, with a combined population representing nearly 40 percent of the total in developing countries. Their combined gross domestic product (GDP) accounts for about three-fifths of the total GDP of developing countries. Appendix I lists the most important of these integration schemes and gives a brief description of each.

THE PROGNOSIS

During the 1970s there has been a spurt of bridge-building activity. Not only has the success of OPEC resulted in vigorous efforts to organize producers' associations, but cooperation has extended to production itself, notably in manufacturing, mining and agriculture. New forms of cooperation are also emerging, such as market sharing arrangements, joint programming and joint ventures. In all these areas progress has been slow for the political and economic reasons touched on above. Meanwhile, for the same variety of reasons, other schemes established before the mid-1960s have either stagnated or disintegrated altogether. In the Latin American Free Trade Association, for instance, the initial growth in trade that resulted from tariff reductions did not lead to more concessions. Reluctance to cut tariffs on nontraditional manufactures was widespread because private enterprises in the member countries were threatened and withdrew their support. In Africa the Council of Entente was made ineffective because, in the general context of low industrialization the industries that emerged had predominant links to developed countries. The East African Community fell apart because Kenya, Tanzania and Uganda were pulling in different directions. In each case the problems are different.

There is no set prescription for success or failure; each situation has its own peculiarities. The outlook, however, is not gloomy. As the 1977 U.N. study referred to earlier noted, "the short time that has elapsed since the formation of most of these associations provides no firm basis for an evaluation of their real impact. In the case of OPEC itself, after all, it required more than a decade for the full benefits of the organization to make themselves felt."

8

Blueprints for Change

When Clausewitz, the 19th century European strategist pointed to the continuum between diplomacy and war he was merely acknowledging an almost self-evident truth. But time, the nuclear bomb, and the growth of a closely interdependent world have broadened the tasks of diplomacy. While it is undoubtedly true that modern diplomats continue to seek advantage for their nations and disadvantage for opponents, it is increasingly recognized that differences cannot be carried to the battlefield without causing general disaster. There is, too, a growing perception that international economic affairs are not, to borrow a phrase from modern mathematics, a "zero sum game." That is to say, one party's benefit is not necessarily another's loss. This perception has been the basis of much development thinking in the past —with transnational corporations, banks and aid agencies arguing that if developed countries profited from aiding in the economic development of poorer countries, it should not be misinterpreted. The difference in the seventies is that developing countries are now using the same argument as they move to assume greater control of their own development. As a result diplomats today are involved in what is surely the greatest task ever attempted by negotiation in history—the redistribution of power without war and the creation of a fair and wholesome world order. They are attempting to change the world's economic structure peacefully, by rational argument; they are trying to reorient the uses of economic and intellectual power. During the present decade this effort has produced a clear picture of the world we inhabit and it would be useful to take stock of it here.

The world today consists of some 150 countries with a population of over 4 billion. These countries and people—all of us without exception—are caught in processes of change that have no precedent in history. We are caught in the full tide of a scientific and technological revolution that is transforming the world before our eyes. We are caught in a demographic boom that will in the foreseeable future double the world's population. Our societies, whether rich or poor, industrialized or agrarian, are all in ferment. Never before have so many millions of people been politically conscious, nor has the exercise of power ever been conditioned, to the extent it is today by popular interest and participation. In every area of human activity change has become the norm, not the exception.

Internationally, we have seen in the last few decades the swift eclipse of colonialism. A few important areas still remain under oppressive foreign rule, but most areas of Africa, Asia and Latin America are now politically free. They are not yet, however, economically independent. Their links to the rich countries of Europe and North America still reflect the old colonial relationship, and this is the starting point of demands for structural change in the world's economy. As colonies, the territories of Africa, Asia and Latin America were developed as appendages of the economies of the ruling countries. They still largely retain their original characteristics of providers of essential primary commodities in exchange for manufactured goods supplied by the industrially developed countries.

The systems of international cooperation set up after the Second World War did little to change the situation. The international monetary system and the agreements that encouraged the vast expansion of world trade in the postwar period paid scant attention to the needs of developing countries. So too with the giant transnational corporations based in developed countries which have been the major agents of economic growth in our time. These corporations are important sources of funds, new technologies, and marketing skills. They control distribution facilities for both primary commodities and manufactured goods. But the strength of these corporations has not contributed to the efforts at economic and social development. In fact they have been a major factor in preserving colonial patterns of production and trade in developing countries.

It is true that the operations of transnational corporations and other private enterprises of developed countries have resulted in a larger volume of production and foreign trade for the host developing countries. However, it is widely recognized that these benefits have been inadequate. The strong bargaining position of the corporations has enabled them to retain a disproportionate share of benefits. Moreover, their investments in developing countries have typically gone for the extraction of raw materials, the manufacture of luxury consumer goods or for the production of labor-intensive export items. This, as well as a range of business practices that tend to stifle local competition and raise prices, have retarded the evolution in developing countries of economic structures necessary to meet the real needs of the population.

Another important factor in world economic relations today is the persistence of close links built up during the colonial period in trade, transport and finance between the developing countries and their former rulers. This has had an adverse effect on the geographical pattern of the external trade of developing countries, for the essential structures for trade among developing countries themselves have been neglected, and consequently such trade has been disproportionately small. Also, trade between developing countries and socialist countries has remained relatively limited. Though expanding fairly rapidly in recent years, it has been confined to a relatively small number of developing countries.

Very briefly, these are the main contours of what we might call the "old international economic order"—the one that exists now, the one the United Nations is committed to change. An integral part of this old order is the existence of a set of iniquitous rules, regulations and customs. These "rules of the game" consist of a complex of intergovernmental treaties, conventions and agreements which collectively serve to facilitate the operations of the private sectors of developed countries. These rules include the basic trading principles of "reciprocity" and "most favored nation" treatment, both enshrined in the General Agreement on Tariffs and Trade (GATT). They include the principle of the sanctity of intellectual property rights as embodied in patents and trademarks and in the freedom of transnational corporations to restrict the use of technology, or to license it with limiting conditions. The rules include also the agreements governing the international monetary system—the creation of new liquidity and the treatment of external debt.

Illustrative of the nature of existing iniquity are the trading arrangements in the world today. When the GATT was negotiated after the Second World War, the main purpose was to free trade from the tangle of prewar restrictions and discriminatory practices. But the two main principles of GATT—"reciprocity" and the "most favored nation" concept—have worked to the disadvantage of developing countries. Reciprocity has meant that unless a country can give a trade concession, it cannot get one, and since the economic weakness of developing countries made it difficult for them to make concessions, they received hardly any. This explains why, after three decades of steadily dismantling tariffs under the aegis of GATT, the exports of developing countries face higher tariff barriers in developed countries than do the exports of developed countries to each other.

The most favored nation principle means that any concessions developing countries agree to exchange even bilaterally, have to be automatically extended to all other GATT members, rich and poor alike. This has, on the one hand, made such exchanges difficult among developing countries by forcing them to compete on equal terms with rich countries. On the other hand, the exchange of concessions among the developed countries has involved products typical of their industrialized economies and thus has not benefited the developing countries. The "generalized system of preferences" proposed by UNCTAD has led to some preferential treatment being given to poorer countries but this has had a rather limited impact. So have recent moves to allow developing countries to give each other preferential treatment. The rules of the game here have quite obviously been written by the rich to suit their own ends.

Underlying such formal principles has been the assumption that the normal operation of market forces would result in an optimal international division of labor, in a rational exploitation of the world's resources, and in a fair sharing of the benefits from international trade. This assumption is now widely questioned. The unregulated operation of market forces has, in fact, been associated with several undesirable trends, including a grossly wasteful use of resources in consumer-oriented developed countries, excessive instability in commodity markets, and large-scale environmental degradation. These trends have led to the realization of the need for a global management of resources. Already the first steps have been taken in this direction in the areas of food supply, industrial production, protection of the environment and rational use of the resources of the sea bed. While it is premature to propose a comprehensive plan for global resource management, such a need must be kept in mind if we are to have a decent and habitable world in the future.

The events of the past decade support the need for drastic changes. The international monetary system, unstable since 1964, broke down completely in 1971. There has been serious inflation globally, and developed capitalist countries in recent years have seen a contraction of economic activity more severe than anything since the 1930s. The action of OPEC in gaining control of a resource on which the entire structure of industrial civilization is dependent has pointed to the limited availability of energy and the need to find new sources. Such new sources of energy will mean change in the ways societies organize production, distribution, transport, and living conditions in general—and thus change in their internal political systems.

The need to protect the environment likewise supports broad change. No longer are environmental concerns seen as merely aesthetic. Scientists are discovering remote and unsuspected implications of our most mundane activities. We could destroy the plankton of the seas—the basis of the marine food chain—by continuing to pump our untreated wastes into rivers; the earth's protective ozone layer far out in the atmosphere could be depleted by the use of fluorocarbon sprays. Politically too, perceptions have been changing. The world has evolved away from the tensions of the cold war, and the expenditure on arms which now totals some four hundred billion dollars a year, seems grossly wasteful in the light of economic and social needs. Yet another element underpinning change is that poorer countries now are not only vocal internationally, but are increasingly powerful economically.

Negotiations on these major issues facing the world community have been in progress—albeit at a painfully slow pace—both within and outside the United Nations. It is within the system, however, that the most intense efforts are being made to reach practical as well as equitable solutions. In this process two resolutions of the U.N. General Assembly have chalked out the main outlines of desired change. The first is the 1974 resolution on the establishment of a New International Economic Order. The second is the Charter of Economic Rights and Duties of States, also adopted in 1974. While the first outlines the main areas and directions of change, the second sets out the principles to be observed in achieving and maintaining a new order. A series of other major world conferences has examined and recommended change in every major area of international relations. The central and guiding concept of all these proposals is that of the need to promote the economic and social progress of developing countries in the context of an expanding world economy. To do so it is essential to reduce and eventually eliminate the economic dependence of developing countries. Particularly important is the reduction of their dependence on the enterprises based in developed countries. Without such independence these countries will not be able to exercise full control over their own natural resources or promote development in directions of their own choosing. A second aim is to accelerate development of the economies of developing countries on the basis of self-reliance. Thirdly, appropriate institutional changes are required to introduce some measure of global management of resources.

Any substantial reduction in the economic dependence of developing countries will involve the regulation of the activities of transnational corporations so as to ensure that they help, not hinder, development efforts. It is important therefore to formulate an internationally acceptable code of conduct for corporations, including rules for the transfer of technology. Such rules are currently being negotiated, and when agreed upon will constitute an essential element in the evolution of a new global order.

There is still much to be done in moving toward the second aim of increasing the collective self-reliance of developing countries. Developing countries need to adopt measures to strengthen their bargaining positions in negotiations, not only with developed countries, but with corporations. If developing countries can bargain on equal terms with these giant companies it is possible that arrangements can be worked out that would benefit all concerned. Other measures of collective action include the pooling of information about sources and costs of available technology; scientific and technological cooperation among themselves; and the establishment of their own production, trading and marketing networks.

It has been recognized by developing countries that what is now required is the elaboration of a comprehensive strategy to strengthen their mutual cooperation in all aspects of economic relations. The command which a group of oil-exporting developing countries have assumed over a larger volume of financial resources provides, for the first time, new opportunities for effective cooperation. The existence in other developing countries of scientific skill and technological know-how, as well as fairly well developed industrial capacities makes self-reliant growth possible. The political processes at work in the world makes it a historical certainty. In this context the 1978 Conference on Technical Cooperation among Developing Countries (TCDC) in Buenos Aires was of considerable significance, for it was there that developing countries moved from rhetorical unity to agreement on several institutional and financial arrangements necessary to encourage greater cooperation among themselves.

9
Setting the Stage

Preparing for a major world conference is a process that seems in the early stages to move in slow motion. Regional meetings are convened in different parts of the world. Experts of many kinds congregate and disperse, leaving studies and reports to mark their passage. Consultations are held among a bewildering variety of organizations and governments. People crisscross the globe carrying documents, making speeches. There is endless talk in committees and working groups as inchoate ideas are traded back and forth with little ostensible effect. But somehow it all works out. As the conference nears, the pace accelerates; a focus emerges, blurred to be sure, but one that draws meaning from the earlier amorphous confusion. Then comes the conference itself and in a few frenzied days the focus assumes a striking clarity. No matter what the subject, the participants discuss the same prime issue: the application of power to achieve solutions. In the end it is always the same. The outcome of the conference is decided by who has the power and how it is shared.

The preparatory process for the TCDC Conference ran true to form. It went on for nearly two years, during which time a small secretariat within the U.N. Development Programme planned and carried out the mandated steps. During 1977 and 1978, with the help of the U.N. Regional Commissions, intergovernmental meetings were held in Bangkok, Lima, Addis Ababa and Kuwait. The problems and potential of TCDC were considered from particular regional viewpoints and an agenda emerged of 102 proposals and recommendations. The Lima meeting also set up a UNDP-supported regional project to identify new methods and procedures to promote TCDC. Following the governmental gathering in Kuwait a panel of experts issued what came to be the much quoted Kuwait Declaration. It said, in part:

Technical Co-operation among Developing Countries (TCDC) is a historical imperative brought about by the need for a new international order. It is a conscious, systematic and politically motivated process developed to create a framework of multiple links between developing countries. Many steps have already been taken in this direction. TCDC may be facilitated, or hindered, but it cannot be stopped.

The process of TCDC cannot be seen in isolation either in space or time. It must be recognized that traditional technical assistance has generally reinforced earlier forms of dependence. This has in effect tended to stifling of self-reliant national capabilities in developing countries. It has also led to incorporating developing countries into a scientific technical and economic system dominated by the highly industrialized world. Such experience has made it evident that self-reliant national capabilities responsive to national objectives and requirements are fundamental prerequisites for viable development.

While this was happening, members of the Conference secretariat circled the globe consulting governments, finding out in detail who thought what. Heading the small staff was the UNDP Administrator in his capacity as Conference Secretary-General, Bradford Morse, a bluff and hearty politician, an ex-member of the U.S. House of Representatives. Next in line for most of the preparatory period was Abdel Razzak Abdel Meguid, an irrepressibly good-humored economist seconded from the ministerial level of the Egyptian government. Under his direction were an Indian, Ambassador Kalyan Vaidya, veteran of many economic negotiations; a Yugoslav, Dusco Dragic; and an Argentinian, Eduardo Albertal. Part of the group, too, but wearing a variety of hats was the Director of the UNDP Information Division, Erskine Childers, who with his Irish gift of blarney popularized the phrase that is used as the title of this book. Together they made a talented top echelon and their efforts produced by September 1977 the first draft of a plan of action. A few months before the Conference, the recall of Abdel Meguid to Egypt to become Planning Minister created a minor crisis. But UNCTAD's Deputy Secretary General, Bernard Chidzero, stepped in and in a few hectic days the draft plan of action was given its final pre-Conference form.

During the preparatory phase governments responded to the U.N. General Assembly's call to prepare their own national reports, focusing on three main aspects of TCDC. These were:

a) the extent and nature of the *experience* of technical cooperation among developing countries so far and the likely degree of participation in future activities;
b) the types of *capacities* available to be used for technical cooperation among developing countries;
c) the volume and types of *needs* that could be met through activities of technical cooperation among developing countries.

Industrialized countries were asked to describe policies and measures adopted for promoting and intensifying TCDC and to give an account of their experiences in supporting TCDC activities. Within countries inter-ministerial committees, professional, technical and voluntary associations engaged in development work cooperated to formulate what would emerge as the national position at the Conference.

As all this information became available it fed into the Preparatory Committee (or "Prep-com" as it was invariably called), an open-ended group of government representatives authorized by the General Assembly to oversee arrangements for the conference. The Prep-com for the TCDC Conference met three times—twice in 1977 and once in 1978. At its second session the Prep-com received two slim but stinging reports. Both were prepared by consultants whose views "did not necessarily reflect those of the Secretariat." Both presented sharp perceptions of reality with none of the usual packing of diplomatic wool. One was titled "Technical Cooperation among Developing Countries as a New Dimension of International Cooperation for Development,"[1] the other "Institutional Arrangements at the International Level to Promote and Conduct Technical Cooperation among Developing Countries."[2] Both were outlines for a fuller presentation under the two main agenda items of the Conference when it met in Buenos Aires in September 1978.

The "New Dimension" outline presented a brief critique of the traditional concept and practice of technical cooperation. Citing a two-volume study[3] on the operations of the U.N. development system, it expressed the view that there was no doubt

> about the heavy bias of the operations of most of the United Nations agencies and institutions toward the wrong notion of superiority of First World knowledge and capital in the context of the development problem of the Third World, and even their bias towards the commercial interests of the First World.

The failure of traditional technical cooperation, it said, had also "revealed itself with dramatic clarity" in the actual performance of most Third World countries during the last three decades. Disillusionment was now widespread, the document said, because traditional technical cooperation had contributed to the growth of mass poverty, the widening of the gap between poor and rich and the frustration of mass initiatives and creativity. It had supported the "growth of foreign controls over key sectors of Third World economies as well as over mass information, economic dependence on few basic exports mostly to developed countries, growing indebtedness and dependency relationships with the centre."

In view of this, the paper went on, it was necessary to "delink" the poorer countries from the dominant rich and "relink" them with each other. The paper pointed out that most of the developing countries were small and poor and had "emerged with distorted social structures from a long period of colonial domination," and fallen into dependency relationships in the world system which were inimical to their development. Most of them could not undertake development in isolation because their resources, institutions and levels of development were inadequate. It was in this context that relinking was necessary and it was here that technical cooperation as a new dimension was of greatest importance.

The paper on institutional arrangements looked at the purposes and the means for this relinking as a threefold process. One was the exchange of knowledge developed or adapted locally by developing countries for the solution of specific development problems. The second was the generation of new knowledge relevant to the conditions prevailing in individual developing countries and specific to their development needs. And the third was to "enable the developing countries to liberate themselves from those links with the developed countries that make for dependency." Institutions for these ends, said the paper, "should be completely controlled and administered by the developing countries concerned and should be almost totally financed by them." Selective use of key inputs from developed countries was not ruled out, but they "should be totally untied and at developing countries' disposal." Involvement by developed countries which was not fully determined by the developing countries carried the danger of converting TCDC into an instrument of dependency, the paper said. Developed countries should have no difficulty in understanding this approach, the paper argued, for their own institutions like the EEC and OECD involved no participants from developing countries.

The paper stressed that TCDC be "need determined." There would be considerable harm, it said, in creating institutions that "seem to compensate for the lack of political will to cooperate as has been the case with a number of institutions of the United Nations system." Because needs were many and varied the institutions too would be diverse. But "no attempt should be made to build up a structure dominated by one or a few apex institutions seeking to control all other institutions lower down in the hierarchy." And networks among existing institutions should be established with the full knowledge that many had "very strong links with developed countries and transnational corporations." At present the success of these institutions depends upon their work being known and accepted by institutions in developed countries where "more than 90% of the research work is undertaken." Linking them all up would not in itself guarantee that they would reorient their thinking and work, the paper warned.

Among the possibilities and examples of institutional arrangements for TCDC the paper presented most of the proposals the Non-Aligned Movement and the Group of 77 had discussed and agreed upon. They included:

- Producer associations on the pattern of OPEC, as well as a Council of Producer Associations.
- Institutions that would help developing countries bargain on an equal level of information and technical competence with transnational corporations.

- Institutions that would help developing countries plan and implement joint agricultural, industrial and marketing ventures.
- Institutions to increase financial cooperation.
- Subregional and regional bodies on the lines of OAU and SELA.
- A full-time secretariat for the Group of 77 or the Non-Aligned Group.

Turning to the participation of the United Nations system, the paper echoed the criticisms in the "New Dimension" paper:

It is well known and widely accepted that the United Nations system is dominated by a few developed countries through their influence on funds, staff and rules and procedures and other practices of the organizations of the United Nations system. There have been even instances of backward linkages of the United Nations system with private enterprises in developed countries. These influences have, by and large, determined the nature and composition of the inputs provided and the knowledge transferred by it. The United Nations system has also shown remarkable resilience against all attempts made so far by the developing countries to reorient it. A few major attempts made recently to restructure the United Nations system have been designed mainly to achieve managerial efficiency and administrative streamlining and to economize on expenditure. These restructuring exercises, instead of trying to change the basic developed-country-oriented outlook of the United Nations system and to reduce their dominance of the system, have had the effect, because of their main emphasis on centralization and managerial streamlining, of further strengthening the grip of these countries on the system.

However, the paper said, the U.N. system did have an important role to play until the developing countries were able to create their own institutional arrangements. The role of the United Nations system would be "one of supporting TCDC activities planned or undertaken by developing countries, suggesting TCDC possibilities through their research activities, narrowing and where possible bridging the information gap." It could also provide a forum for the exchange of experience and facilitate the political processes of cooperation among developing countries. The U.N. Development Programme was in a "particularly advantageous position to play a catalytic role in promoting TCDC" for it had "accumulated operational experience, expert field staff and a wide network of resident representatives in developing countries." This was why, the paper noted, the central role in promoting TCDC has been assigned by the General Assembly to UNDP.

Looking to the future development of the U.N. development system, the paper saw the need to make TCDC its principal vocation.

There is a strong and widely respected section of opinion which believes that the United Nations development system has until now been utilized by the developed countries for furthering their own development objectives. Is it not now the time to allow the developing countries to utilize it for their development purposes?

In this connection it recalled the comment of Dr. I.G. Patel, UNDP Deputy Administrator, who told the ESCAP regional TCDC meeting:

> ... Equality if not preference demands that if bilateral assistance is tied to inputs from richer countries, multilateral assistance should be tied to inputs from poorer countries.

Mr. Bradford Morse, the Administrator of UNDP, had also repeatedly "asserted that he intends to make TCDC the major goal and central objective of UNDP," the paper said. The logical conclusion from this, it argued, could "well be to transform UNDP and the United Nations development system along with it, primarily into a TCDC organization." However, as the developing countries would continue to be in need of the transfer from developed countries of relevant knowledge and equipment, the United Nations system should continue to conduct technical co-operation among developed and developing countries on a highly selective basis and as a subsidiary activity.

The advice of the two strident papers made little impression on the Prepcom's recommendations. In May 1978 it recommended for the Conference a provisional agenda with two substantive items:

1. Technical cooperation among developing countries as a new dimension of international cooperation for development—
   a) TCDC and its interrelationship with economic, scientific, social and cultural cooperation among developing countries;
   b) TCDC as a means of enhancing the availability and effectiveness of development resources for international cooperation and its inter-relationship with over-all international cooperation;
   c) The role of TCDC in exploring new approaches and strategies for solving development problems common to developing countries;
   d) Expansion of the participation in TCDC of the least developed and geographically disadvantaged countries;
   e) Measures for enhancing confidence in the existing and potential capabilities of developing countries for mutual technical coopera-tion;
   f) Development and operation of an action-oriented information system on the technical capacities available in developing countries for use by other developing countries;
   g) Identification of existing and possible sources and methods of financing TCDC;
   h) Measures for stimulating and strengthening consultancy, engineer-ing and other technical services as well as the supply and procure-ment of such services and of equipment and materials of developing countries through the promotion of TCDC;
   i) Measures for reducing, through the promotion of TCDC, the "brain drain" affecting developing countries;

j) Development of a comprehensive public information and educational program designed to make the importance and nature of TCDC better known, and particularly the role to be played therein by both public and private sectors;

k) Institutional arrangements at the national level to promote and conduct TCDC, including administrative, legal and financial arrangements and participation of public and private sectors; and

l) Institutional arrangements at the international level to promote and conduct TCDC and the participation of developed countries, the United Nations system, and other international organizations; and

2. Adoption of a plan of action for promoting and implementing TCDC.

The stage was set for Buenos Aires, the props were ready. What the actors did with them is the theme of the next chapter.

10

The Conference

The conference met in the San Martin Cultural Centre, a complex of small and large auditoriums usually given over to the many drama troupes of Buenos Aires. It was not an altogether inappropriate site; the conference filled the halls with its own complex drama. This did not involve the fireworks of North-South confrontation characteristic of the seventies; in fact there was little of angry declamation or even eloquence, for the conference differed significantly in nature and aim from other recent world meetings. It was, for one thing, a conference where the real work of agreement lay among developing countries themselves. Developed countries had, at best, a supporting role. In recognition of this they had sent fairly low level representatives, ambassadors and civil servants, while developing countries sent people who made decisions at or near the cabinet level. Most of these were economic planners.

The conference opened without the usual fanfare of rhetorical trumpets. Argentinian President Jorge Rafael Videla made a brief, almost perfunctory speech, stressing the brotherhood of man. He announced, without giving details, that Argentina would set up a fund for promoting TCDC. Following him, U.N. Secretary-General Kurt Waldheim made a businesslike statement putting the U.N. role in perspective. The Conference, he said, was the "most recent demonstration of the United Nations effort to help find solutions to the interlocking problems of our interdependent world." The previous conferences the United Nations had sponsored in recent years "including those on environment, population, food, desertification, human settlements, water—even as this one on technical cooperation among developing countries—must not be looked at in isolation." Each formed "part of new global strategies to cope with global problems that affect all of us. Each draws and builds upon its predecessors, just as the United Nations Conference on Science and Technology for Development next year will undoubtedly benefit from and, as appropriate, absorb the results of this conference."

Putting the Conference in the context of work towards a new international economic order, Mr. Waldheim said that "year by year the interdependence of all national economies is becoming more and more evident." Millions of jobs in the developed countries existed "because of their trade with the developing countries, which provide many of the natural resources and commodities essential for industrialized economies." There should be, he said, "no doubt of the need for fair and stable but periodically adjustable terms being accorded these critical exports. But the developing countries must also expand cooperation among themselves in order fully to provide for the coming massive demand from their own growing populations, and they must have a larger role as exporters of processed and manufactured products." However, he added, "with such an increased global demand, the share of that demand for exports from developed countries also cannot be in doubt." The growing economic interdependence of the world, Mr. Waldheim said, was demonstrated by the TCDC Conference symbol, depicting as it did, not only a bridge but vertical lines linking the northern and southern hemispheres.

It was clear, Mr. Waldheim went on, that TCDC was "not the exclusive possession of the United Nations development system." While the system should stand ready to provide support and assistance as and when requested, it was the "sovereign prerogative of every developing country to determine its relationships and modalities of co-operation with other developing countries." It was clear though that developing countries did wish to see an expanded U.N. role in supporting TCDC. The draft Plan of Action submitted to the Conference reflected the Secretariat's efforts to suggest what these continued roles would involve, taking into account the extensive comments of governments in the preparatory committee.

Speaking later that afternoon the Conference Secretary-General Bradford Morse went into greater detail on the results of the preparatory process. It had become clear, he said, that "on the one hand TCDC should be devoted to the enhancement of national development based more securely in self-reliance, and to the expanded use of developing countries' resources in skills, training, and equipment and on the other that TCDC should be employed to help advance the establishment of the new international economic order." Elaborating on this dual role Mr. Morse said that "by its very nature TCDC is already, and will certainly to an even greater extent, be involved in both dimensions." The uses of TCDC were for each sovereign government to decide, he said. The modalities and channels for use of TCDC might vary according to the dimension to which it was applied, but he hoped that there was a "common understanding that there is no need for an 'either-or' approach to these dimensions." For example, he went on, the United Nations Development Programme and other UN specialized agencies were supporting TCDC projects in such national efforts as fisheries development and health infrastructure, as well as projects to strengthen the secretariats of commodity producers' associations and skills of officials engaged in multinational trade negotiations. "The challenge is how to use TCDC to move forward in all dimensions of development and economic relations, which are in any case inextricably intertwined. Surely one of the major new perspectives that is present at this conference is this interdependence of forces between internal national development and the external, international economic order." To nourish one with TCDC and starve the other of its potential would make little sense.

According to all the evidence available to the Secretariat from the Prepcom sessions and from innumerable consultations, Mr. Morse continued,

> The developing countries wished this conference to be a full United Nations world conference because there was no intention to create some barrier between TCDC and technical cooperation as presently organized through multilateral United Nations channels and historical bilateral cooperation. On the contrary, I believe that all of us, from all regions of the world, hope that TCDC and traditional technical cooperation will be complementary; and especially that TCDC, as it enhances self-reliance, will help ensure that technical cooperation with developed countries will be even more effective, more cost beneficial and more usefully and carefully chosen for those resources that can best come from developed countries.

Turning to the draft plan of action submitted by the Secretariat, Mr. Morse said that it did not specify "priorities for action among the different and enormous needs of the developing countries." But he would like to suggest that the critical ingredients of success lay in answers to three questions. These were:

- What concrete action will advance the use of TCDC, for solution of which specific development and cooperation needs?
- How may additional resources for such specific action be mobilized?
- What machinery do governments feel may be most effective to ensure that the implementation of the resolutions of this Conference can be reviewed and new policies debated and determined?

The Conference moved swiftly to work after the opening ceremonies, setting up a committee to consider the draft Plan of Action while a general debate was held in plenary. The first speaker in the debate was the man elected to chair the main committee—Abdel Razzak Abdel Meguid, the 47-year-old Egyptian economist and Minister for Planning who three months previously had been in effective charge of the Conference secretariat. He was to play a key role in the next two weeks and his initial statement indicated the main direction of his effort.

> The problem we are meeting to consider today is not a new one. Nor is the perception of it unique to our troubled times. This meeting comes in a line of international gatherings aimed at improving the world development system and international cooperation. Indeed one may be struck by the similarity of the expressions used, the family resemblance of the proposals made in New Delhi, Cairo, Bandung, Algiers, Dakar, Kuwait, Libreville,

Mexico and Khartoum. During the last three decades we have identified the changing nature of the problems that afflict the world; we have even had a fair approximation of what needs to be done—culminating in the Declaration of the U.N. General Assembly issued in 1974 calling for a New International Economic Order. After four years of negotiations and some ad hoc action, little favorable results, not quite adequate to the tasks at hand, have been achieved.

Analyzing this failure, Mr. Meguid said it "would not be contrary to our values and tradition to start our debate with a note of understanding, perhaps sympathy, with the position of developed countries." The stage of economic development, characterized by mass consumption, which had been reached by most advanced nations was showing signs of great stress and instability, he said.

This instability is reflected in a number of serious contradictions which are plaguing advanced societies. Inflation which in a real sense signifies excessive demand for resources exists side by side with unemployed resources . . . of people and of factories. To safeguard the interests of their people, individual developed countries have been forced to raise economic curtains around their borders. The intensified and free flow of international trade which has been the engine of growth since the Second World War is not today being fully utilized. The result is monetary instability, high levels of unemployment, recession, stagnation, balance of payments problems and other symptoms which are socially and politically disturbing for the developed countries themselves. The reactions by developed countries in the form of lower growth targets, of trade restrictions and overall retrenchment, explainable in the short term and for a few individual countries, is unfortunately intensifying the global disequilibrium.

This was happening, he went on, at a time when developing countries themselves, having accelerated their development efforts over the past three decades, were in a position to play their role in the international economic community, not just as recipients of aid and providers of raw materials, but as true partners in the exchange of goods, technology and skills on an equitable and just basis.

Determined politically to utilize the engine of growth, which was well served by free international trade flows in the past, developing countries' efforts are becoming increasingly frustrated by the barriers raised around what has been their traditional markets and partners.

They were witnessing the erosion of this partnership, said Mr. Meguid.

The emergence of this global disequilibrium should not be seen as necessarily stemming from any lack of goodwill or from deliberate attempts to disrupt the world economy, Mr. Meguid went on.

Rather it has come about as a logical result of forces within and reactions by individual or groups of countries over a turbulent period of economic events. Hence the need for a new dimension in international cooperation. It is in this context that this conference on TCDC is important, at least for three main reasons. First, it provides an opportunity to reach international agreement on *practical* lines of action to initiate and strengthen cooperation among developing countries in many critical fields.

Second, the conference has real *political* significance, in demonstrating the solidarity, the conviction and the common interest of the world community as a whole in recognizing that the time has come to open up a whole new dimension of international cooperation.

Third, the conference has real *moral and psychological* importance in changing the way in which we view the world. It should lead to the recognition throughout the world of the determination and capability of the developing countries to shape their futures.

In the work of restructuring the international economy, Mr. Meguid said, the developed countries had their own institutions for cooperation while the poorer countries had none. "Those of us, and there are many here, who deal, day by day, with the practical problems of initiating, encouraging and sustaining the development efforts of our countries, are well aware of the difficulties to be overcome in our efforts to strengthen self-reliance and cooperation among our countries." Developing countries could and did make bilateral and even regional arrangements. But these needed to be broadened if all the latent strength of Africa, Asia and Latin America was to be fully used. The Conference, Mr. Meguid concluded, must "develop a range of recommendations aimed at ensuring that TCDC becomes properly integrated throughout the bilateral and multilateral global systems."

The debate that Mr. Meguid initiated continued for a week in the plenary. Some 150 speakers were heard, most of them from the 138 countries represented at the conference and the rest from a wide range of international organizations. As debates go it was a tame affair, showing, as the Austrian speaker noted on the fourth day, "a wide convergence of views on the basic features of TCDC." But there was some cut and thrust along the way, albeit phrased so diplomatically that one had to know the code to understand the argument. When, for instance, the representative of a developed country pointed to the "attitudinal barriers" to TCDC and said in a seeming non sequitur that their removal would involve facing up to the problem of "how the benefits of TCDC can be spread beyond the relatively small number of developing countries which currently possess the capacity to provide services and other inputs on a significant scale," he was scoring a debating point. In the press room outside the same point was being consistently raised by Western correspondents when they asked whether TCDC would not lead to the "exploitation" of the poorest countries by the more industrialized among them. It was essentially an attack on the unity of the poorer countries, an attempt to reinforce attitudinal barriers among them by encouraging mistrust. The response from the developing countries involved continually stressing their unity and the democratic, voluntary and mutually beneficial potential for TCDC.

Generally, the positions of developed countries were supportive of TCDC and there were good economic reasons for this. One was the expectation that if developing countries found new markets for their manufactured goods, the pressure would ease on developed countries to increase such cheap imports. Another reason was that in many cases TCDC would mean increased business for transnational corporations. As Dusco Dragic, the Director in charge of UNDP's Information Referral System (INRES) told a meeting of the TCDC Workshop,[1] "at least half of the consultancy services listed in INRES are not genuine developing country concerns." They were, he said, branches of services with headquarters in developed countries. Yet another reason was that TCDC activities, especially in creating basic infrastructures for transport and communications, would open up possibilities for Western business investments. Other reasons for support were of course the often repeated commitment to aid economic and social development and the perception of TCDC as a new and valuable means to increase the effectiveness of international efforts.

Support from the developed countries for TCDC was a running theme of the debate. Such support, as the Jamaican speaker pointed out, was already being provided by "enlightened" developed countries.

We believe there are some developed countries which are ready to enter into such arrangements without attempting to use the incentive of financing to distort the project from its original objectives. . . . Jamaica believes that without such enlightened assistance the tasks facing the developing countries will be rendered immeasurably more difficult. We therefore request that the programmes of activities already being pursued be used as the framework into which such resources and any new ones which might be contributed should be channelled. At the same time any moves by donor countries to untie their assistance for TCDC and allow consultants and materials to be procured from other developing countries will have a multiplying effect on the value of such assistance and be fully in the spirit of TCDC.

Delegation after delegation from developing countries echoed the view—existing north-south flows and TCDC should not be in conflict; they were complementary.

Socialist countries, too, had a running theme—that disarmament and a decrease in international tensions were necessary for the success of TCDC. The Soviet Union's ambassador pointed out that the daily global expenditure on arms—over one billion dollars—was more than a year's outlay by the entire U.N. system on technical cooperation. Another recurring point made by speakers from socialist countries was that they objected to being put in the same class as developed capitalist countries when "North-South" issues were being discussed.

Socialist states supported TCDC, but it was not a blanket approval. As the speaker from the German Democratic Republic put it, his country would "encourage and support all progressive elements of technical cooperation among developing countries." The German Democratic Republic would "take into account, within its possibilities, the processes and requirements connected with TCDC for the planned development of its relations to the developing countries. Having in mind the principles of equality and mutual advantage we are convinced that at the same time TCDC should open up new sources in order to expand relations between the developing countries and the German Democratic Republic as well as the other socialist states and to promote mutual exchanges." The representative of Poland pointed out that the experience of the socialist countries "both in the area of socioeconomic development of individual states and in the field of cooperation within the socialist coummunity" was "especially valuable" to developing countries and for TCDC in particular. "Many of the socialist countries not so long ago had to solve similar problems with which the developing countries are confronted today."

The main focus of the debate, however, was not on the relations between the different groups of countries, but on relations among developing countries, the forms of TCDC, its present status and potential. It was widely recognized, as the speaker from Bangladesh put it, that "TCDC despite its great appeal is still a very small element in intercountry economic relations." The reasons, he said, "are three major barriers—informational gaps, attitudinal impediments and financial difficulties." If the conference served to overcome these difficulties in some measure it would have succeeded.

The Nigerian speaker emphasized the importance of "building TCDC on sound foundations." It was "not by accident" he said, that a majority of the cases where TCDC had been successful was between contiguous countries or among countries of a region. For global TCDC to succeed "steps should be taken to strengthen the existing bilateral, subregional and regional activities and organizations." Africa, he said, needed TCDC in addition to traditional forms of technical cooperation because in it were the majority of the world's least developed and land-locked countries. It was this recognition that had led two summit meetings of the Organization of African Unity (OAU), in 1977 in Libreville and in 1978 in Khartoum, to affirm support for the TCDC Conference and its basic objectives.

The leader of the Indian delegation summed up the broad objectives and principles of TCDC under nine heads:

(1) TCDC must be a collective effort, and should be based on the principle of universality. The whole purpose of TCDC would be defeated, if there is any feeling or apprehension anywhere that the movement would be to the disadvantage of any or to the benefit of a few. There is a role to be played by all countries including developed ones.

(2) TCDC must be a two-way traffic. It will only succeed if it is based on genuine reciprocity and mutuality of benefit. While there should be readiness on the part of those who are more advantageously placed to make their services available for those who are not, there should be no donor-recipient relationship of the traditional type and exchanges must be on the basis of genuine equality.

(3) TCDC must promote and accelerate the use of appropriate technologies for development in developing countries.

(4) The new movement must take special care to ensure that experts sent to give technical aid or impart training try to identify themselves with the people of the country to which they go and their problems, and devise solutions appropriate to their conditions.

(5) TCDC is an additional instrument for dealing with the problems of development and enhancing technical capacities. It cannot, therefore, be a substitute for traditional technical cooperation. It must supplement existing exchanges and cooperation.

(6) TCDC should function within the framework of the development plans and programmes of participant countries. It must not create, lead to or strengthen separate economic interests or dual or multiple economic systems.

(7) TCDC should be based on scrupulous regard for the different socioeconomic and national personalities of the participant countries.

(8) TCDC should aim at creating and developing indigenous capacity to respond to developmental problems thereby enhancing national self-reliance.

(9) TCDC should encourage collective research and the application of the results of such research in areas and fields of common concern, e.g., public health, social welfare, education, technical training, etc.

These principles and aims were also stated by many others, but, as the Indonesian speaker pointed out, "however lofty ideals are, in the final analysis it is the implementation that really matters." The debate turned on the issue of how TCDC would be implemented. What mechanisms would be created for it, how would existing structures adapt? The Indonesian views on these matters reflected those of the great majority: "We should make full use of the mechanism and arrangements now available to us, particularly in the U.N. system in preference to a new one. They are, of course, open for improvement in order to enable them to cope with the expanding cooperation envisaged in the plan of action."

There was no disagreement either when the Argentinian delegation said that three types of organizations were capable of implementing TCDC—private organizations, national institutions (such as universities and public sector undertakings), and international organizations. Each type of organization had special areas of capability—trade, intellectual and cultural relationships, problems of overall economic relations. But differences emerged on what type of arrangements should be made at the international level. The Dutch spokesman reflected the position of most developed countries when he said that all units of the U.N. development system "share a common concern for the acceleration of the process towards self-reliance; all should thus share a common responsibility for the promotion of TCDC, each organization within its own sphere of competence and interest." There was, he added, no need for the "establishment of an intergovernmental machinery with exclusive title to the promotion of TCDC." Developing countries, however, believed that unless there was some central overseeing and policy-making body, the U.N. system would not really pick up its socks.

While the debate in the plenary served to record the differing positions of countries, the main committee was working furiously in the interests of consensus, to change them. In a group chaired by one of the committee vice-chairmen, Benjamin Bassin of Finland, the Plan of Action was being negotiated paragraph by paragraph. The procedure was for the Group of 77 to caucus first, reach an agreed position, and then present it to the working group. The most important step was the first—reaching an agreed 77 position. "I would say it took about two-thirds of the time we spent in negotiating the draft plan," said one of the key negotiators, Arundhati Ghose of India. By Saturday, September 9, the process was almost complete when the Chairman of the Group of 77, Frank Francis of Jamaica, met the press to report on progress. A lank light-brown man with graying curly hair and an easy, almost throw-away manner of speech, he was limp with fatigue, having worked through most of the preceding two nights. There had been "intensive negotiations" on Thursday and Friday, he said. These involved countries of all groups, although "other groups were not working in a very co-ordinated manner." There was, he said, no strictly unified position of developed countries on any of the major issues. Nor was there any "massive struggle between developed and developing countries on the issue of financial resources." Negotiations had dealt with the "innumerable details of the Plan of Action, focussing most significantly on "certain central arrangements. We do not have the impression that any delegation is opposed to the organizational need to consider TCDC at a high level," Mr. Francis said. "The debate here and the negotiations are on the details of how to do this."

The details centered around Recommendation 36 of the draft Plan of Action, the one titled "Intergovernmental Machinery." It called upon the General Assembly to "entrust an intergovernmental machinery with the responsibility for monitoring and reviewing the progress made in implementing the adopted Plan of Action." Further, it would act to strengthen TCDC, promote new and innovative policies, "consider the availability" of financial resources and "ensure co-ordination" of TCDC activities by the U.N. system. The draft suggested that the proposed machinery could take the form of a "committee on TCDC of the Governing Council of UNDP, which would be open to all states and would report through the Governing Council and the Economic and Social Council to the United Nations General Assembly." The developing countries did not like the terms of reference suggested by the plan or the position offered the new body as a committee of the UNDP Council; developed countries generally approved of both. At issue was power, the long-term control of the U.N. Development Programme, and to understand it we must look to the origins and growth of the U.N. development system.

The concepts of international economic cooperation that guided the creation of the U.N. development system were born in the experience of wartime alliances and postwar reconstruction. During the war there had been a pooling among the victorious Allies of raw materials and transport, of military equipment and financial resources—and this was a rigorously planned exercise. After the war the massive effort at reconstruction involved more planning and coordination. As U.N. Secretary-General Waldheim noted, this experience influenced development efforts. "The tendency to assume that development almost automatically meant external assistance from developed countries derived in part from the emergency nature of the massive post-war relief and development programmes which necessarily involved outside aid and technical assistance from richer countries to poorer ones."

Another heritage of the war was the importance given to the "great powers," even in matters of economic and social development—a context in which developing countries should logically have had the main role in deciding what they wanted done. Instead the "great powers" dominated the process by which the U.N. system of specialized agencies was set up, and the result was that only the World Bank was given a strong operational role. Organizations like UNESCO, ILO, FAO, etc. were meant mainly "as clearing houses of information designed primarily to organize international cooperation, harmonize policy, promote research and set standards in their respective fields rather than (WHO excepted) engage in operational activities."[2] The World Bank, as we have seen, has always been controlled by a few developed countries, its lending policies restricted to development projects profitable enough to repay loans and interest in hard currencies.

During the 1950s developing countries pushed for an organization that would provide money and technical assistance on less stringent terms. They proposed in the U.N. General Assembly for a Special U.N. Fund for Economic Development (SUNFED) which would not be confined to any kind of assistance in particular but would provide whatever was necessary for development. As Michael Geoghegan notes in "Third World and Global Society," the major financing countries of the West opposed the idea because they did not want "an institution sponsored by the General Assembly and one which they would no longer control."[3] In particular they did not want anything that would compete with the World Bank in providing capital for development. Socialist countries supported the demands of developing countries but offered no money. Over the years that followed, as developing countries grew ever more insistent, the richer countries acceded to the creation in 1965 of the U.N. Development Programme. The UNDP brought together two older programs for technical assistance; its main intent was preinvestment aid to help poor countries prepare for larger and more productive capital investments from abroad or within its borders. Rich countries still retained control of the process, however, for the new UNDP's policy-making Governing Council was split almost equally between developed and developing countries and its operations depended on money contributed annually by the richer states.

It was this element of control that the TCDC Conference focused upon.

In a world where developing countries increasingly had the technical and financial resources to help themselves, UNDP's control mechanisms were anachronistic. Efforts at change took three lines—one on "intergovernmental machinery," another on "financial arrangements," and the third on "strengthening the capacity of UNDP for the promotion and support of TCDC." On the first, the conference recommended that, in view of the UNDP's central role in technical assistance, the overall intergovernmental review of TCDC within the UN system should be "entrusted by the General Assembly to a high-level meeting of all States participating in the UNDP." This meeting would be convened by the UNDP Administrator and would, after annual meetings in 1980 and 1981, be held biennially. They would convene in the same place as, and prior to, sessions of the UNDP Governing Council and would carry out the following functions:

(a) Review the progress made in implementing the tasks entrusted to the United Nations development system by the Buenos Aires Plan of Action;
(b) Ensure that efforts to strengthen TCDC are sustained within the U.N. development system;
(c) Support new policies and innovative approaches to further the development of TCDC;
(d) Consider the availability of financial resources and their effective use by the United Nations development system, without prejudice to existing programs;
(e) Ensure coordination of the promotional and operational TCDC activities of the United Nations development system.

The Conference called upon "United Nations organs, organizations and bodies, including the regional commissions, and other subregional, regional and interregional intergovernmental organizations" to participate actively in the work of these meetings. The meetings would report to the U.N. General Assembly through the UNDP Governing Council and the Economic and Social Council.

By creating this new body the conference put in place the means by which UNDP could change gracefully as world realities changed. Briefing correspondents on the matter, the Chairman of the Main Committee, Mr. Meguid, compared the arrangement to one that already existed at the World Bank and the International Monetary Fund which he said were the "most undemocratic" units of the U.N. system. By charter, their executive and policy power was in the hands of a small group of Executive Directors, most of them representing the developed countries. But every year the Bank and the Fund had a joint meeting of all member states and in recent years these annual meetings had succeeded in initiating changes and policies that reflected the broader interests of developing countries. Similarly, he hoped, the new high-level meetings of all states called for in the Plan of Action would have a positive impact on the formulation and implementation of TCDC policies. Supporting the transition within UNDP would be a strengthened "special unit" for TCDC. It would serve essentially as the secretariat for the new intergovernmental body, "arranging for the necessary studies and analyses to be undertaken and submitted to the governments for consideration and approval." It would cooperate with all units of the U.N. development system in helping governments join in TCDC and coordinate the relevant UNDP activities. It would expand, strengthen and promote the efficient use of the International Reference Service (INRES). And, perhaps most importantly, the unit was asked to help in "preparing modifications in the policies, rules and procedures of UNDP" to promote TCDC.

The recommendation on financial arrangements marked another important step toward the reform of UNDP. As its preamble stated: "In view of the fact that the financing of TCDC activities is primarily the responsibility of developing countries themselves, it will nevertheless be necessary for the developed countries and the United Nations development system to support these activities financially without prejudice to the decision-making control by the developing countries of these TCDC activities." Among the 10 subparagraphs that followed, four were of particular significance:

> Developing countries which may wish to do so should consider earmarking a percentage of their Indicative Planning Figure (IPF)[4] of UNDP at the national level, for financing TCDC projects at the bilateral and subregional levels;
>
> Regional IPFs or UNDP should be used to the maximum possible extent on the basis of regional priorities, for financing TCDC projects and activities. The responsibility for identifying and initiating such projects and activities should lie with the developing countries of the region concerned;
>
> A sizable proportion of interregional and global IPFs of UNDP should be devoted to the financing of TCDC projects and activities requested by two or more developing countries of different regions. The management of these resources should be conducted in close consultation with the developing countries concerned;
>
> All organizations of the U.N. development system should allocate an increasing proportion of their resources for TCDC activities and projects. (See table 10.1.)

In the original position paper of the Group of 77 on financing, it had been agreed that all regional and global IPFs should be devoted to TCDC activities. Even if this was changed later in negotiations with the developed countries, its implication was not lost: a great attitudinal barrier had, officially, been removed. It was a statement of confidence in the concept and potential of collective self-reliance.

After the resolution of these controversial issues, the rest of the plan fell easily into shape. Before the scheduled end of the conference the plan was ready, a 65-paragraph document with 38 recommendations. The first 14 of these dealt with national action; the next seven with subregional and

Table 10.1 UNDP: Indicative Planning Figures for the First and Second Cycles 1972–76 and 1977–81 (thousands of dollars)

	IPF 1972–76	IPF 1977–81		IPF 1972–76	IPF 1977–81
Afghanistan	20,000	38,000	Mexico	20,000	20,000
Albania	1,000	4,250	Mongolia	10,000	10,000
Algeria	20,000	20,000	Morocco	20,000	20,000
Angola	3,000	10,950	Mozambique	4,500	19,000
Argentina	20,000	20,000	Namibia	1,000	4,750
Bahrain	2,500	2,500	Nepal	15,000	32,500
Bangladesh	18,500	65,500	Nicaragua	5,000	5,000
Barbados	2,500	2,500	Niger	10,000	19,750
Belize	1,000	1,000	Nigeria	30,000	45,500
Benin	7,500	16,250	Niue	a	1,000
Bhutan	2,500	12,250	Oman	a	4,000
Bolivia	15,000	15,500	Pakistan	18,500	52,500
Botswana	5,800	8,500	Panama	7,500	7,500
Brazil	30,000	30,000	Papua New Guinea	5,000	8,750
Bulgaria	7,500	7,500	Paraguay	7,500	7,500
Burma	15,000	41,500	Peru	15,000	15,000
Burundi	10,000	18,750	Philippines	20,000	30,500
Cape Verde	1,500	4,000	Poland	7,500	7,500
Central African Empire	7,500	11,750	Portugal	—	4,000
Chad	7,500	19,000	Qatar	1,500	c
Chile	20,000	20,000	Republic of Korea	15,000	18,000
Colombia	20,000	20,000	Romania	7,500	7,500
Comoros	a	7,200	Rwanda	10,000	19,750
Congo	7,500	7,500	Samoa	5,000	5,250

Table 10.1 (Cont.) UNDP: Indicative Planning Figures for the First and Second Cycles 1972–76 and 1977–81 (thousands of dollars)

	IPF 1972–76	IPF 1977–81		IPF 1972–76	IPF 1977–81
Costa Rica	5,000	5,000	Sao Tome and Principe	500	1,500
Cuba	10,000	13,500	Saudi Arabia	10,000	10,000
Cyprus	5,000	5,000	Senegal	10,000	11,750
Czechoslovakia	2,500	2,500	Seychelles	a	1,600
Democratic Kampuchea	10,000	25,500	Sierra Leone	7,500	13,250
Democratic Yemen	10,000	14,500	Singapore	7,500	7,500
Djibouti	a	850	Solomon Islands	1,000	2,300
Dominican Republic	7,500	7,500	Somalia	15,000	18,250
Ecuador	15,000	15,000	Spain	5,000	c
Egypt	27,500	31,500	Sri Lanka	15,000	31,500
El Salvador	5,000	9,250	Sudan	20,000	33,000
Equatorial Guinea	3,500	4,000	Surinam	2,500	3,500
Ethiopia	20,000	42,000	Swaziland	5,700	5,750
Fiji	5,000	5,000	Syrian Arab Republic	15,000	15,000
Gabon	7,500	7,500	Thailand	15,000	29,500
Gambia	2,500	7,000	Togo	10,000	11,000
Ghana	15,000	19,000	Tonga	1,000	2,000
Gilbert Islands	500d	550	Trinidad and Tobago	5,000	5,000
Greece	7,500	7,500	Trust Territory of the Pacific Is.	a	1,000
Guatemala	7,500	7,500	Tunisia	15,000	15,000
Guinea	15,000	21,750	Turkey	20,000	20,000
Guinea-Bissau	2,500	5,750	Tuvalu	d	550
Guyana	5,000	5,000	Uganda	10,000	30,000

Table 10.1 (Cont.) UNDP: Indicative Planning Figures for the First and Second Cycles 1972–76 and 1977–81
(thousands of dollars)

	IPF 1972–76	IPF 1977–81
Haiti	6,000	18,750
Honduras	5,000	9,250
Hong Kong	500	500
Hungary	7,500	3,500[c]
Iceland	1,000	c
India	50,000	97,000
Indonesia	35,000	69,500
Iran	20,000	20,000
Iraq	15,000	15,000
Israel	5,000	c
Ivory Coast	15,000	15,000
Jamaica	7,500	7,500
Jordan	15,000	15,000
Kenya	15,000	27,500
Kuwait	1,000	c
Lao People's Democratic Republic	5,000	17,750
Lebanon	10,000	10,000
Lesotho	8,300	13,250
Liberia	10,000	10,000
Libyan Arab Jamahiriya	5,000	5,000
Madagascar	10,000	23,750
Malawi	7,500	19,750
Malaysia	15,000	15,000
United Arab Emirates	a	1,000
United Republic of Cameroon	15,000	17,250
United Republic of Tanzania	15,000	33,500
Upper Volta	10,700	23,750
Uruguay	10,000	10,000
Venezuela	10,000	10,000
Viet Nam	10,000	44,000
Yemen	15,000	23,750
Yugoslavia	7,500	7,500
Zaire	20,000	34,500
Zambia	15,000	15,000
Undistributed Africa	2,000	—
Undistributed Asia and the Pacific	2,500	3,800
Undistributed Europe, Mediterranean and the Middle East	5,000	—
Undistributed Latin America	15,000	21,550
National Liberation Movements[b]	—	6,000
Future Participants, etc.	—	55,850
Regional Africa	71,200	105,900
Regional Asia and the Pacific	40,700	95,700
Regional Europe, Mediterranean and the Middle East	19,700	44,300
Regional Latin America	61,500	63,000

Table 10.1 (Cont.) UNDP: Indicative Planning Figures for the First and Second Cycles
1972–76 and 1977–81
(thousands of dollars)

	IPF 1972–76	IPF 1977–81		IPF 1972–76	IPF 1977–81
Maldives	1,000	2,500	Interregional	22,400	30,100
Mali	10,000	24,000	Global	15,500	50,200
Malta	2,500	2,500			
Mauritania	5,000	9,750	Total	1,537,500	2,454,900
Mauritius	5,000	5,250			

[a]Included under Undistributed.
[b]National Liberation Movements recognized by the Organization of African Unity in accordance with the relevant decisions of the UNDP Governing Council.
[c]These countries have partially or wholly relinquished their IPFs.
[d]Refers to Gilbert and Ellice Islands.

regional activity; one with action at the interregional level, and the final 16 with global action. The thrust of it all was summed up in the introduction, part of which read as follows:

> Profound changes are taking place in international political and economic relationships. When the principal institutions of the present international system were first established, a group of industrialized countries were dominant in world affairs. However, the historic process of decolonization now makes it possible for a large number of States, representing an overwhelming proportion of the world's population, to participate in international affairs. Moreover, substantial changes are taking place at the world level in the control and distribution of resources and in the capabilities and needs of nations. As a result of these changes and other international developments, the expansion of international relations and co-operation and the interdependence of nations are progressively increasing. Interdependence, however, demands sovereign and equal participation in the conduct of international relations and the equitable distribution of benefits.
>
> The international system is in a state of ferment. Concepts, political and economic positions, institutions and relationships must be adjusted to the new realities and changing perceptions. It is in this perspective that the countries of the developing world have made their call for the new international economic order as an expression of their political will and their determination, based on the principles of national and collective self-reliance, to work towards a new pattern of international relations more appropriate to the real circumstances and reflecting fully the interests of the world community as a whole.

With the adoption of the plan the Conference was judged a major success. An "important event in contemporary history," said the African spokesman. A "miracle of consensus," said the speaker for the Asian group. A "resounding success," agreed the representative of the West Europeans. Unlike the other conferences convened since the call for a new international economic order by the U.N. General Assembly in 1974, this one had not disappointed hopes. "We have, in fact, surprised ourselves by what we have achieved," said Bradford Morse.

There was only one sour note as the Conference ended: news from New York about the collapse of talks in the "Committee of the Whole." The Committee, set up by the General Assembly in 1977, was meant to be the central U.N. mechanism to help negotiations toward a new international economic order. By September 1978, however, the Committee had not yet agreed on the nature of its own mandate. Developing countries believed the Committee had power to negotiate in the event of deadlock in any other forum; Western countries had seemed on the point of agreeing with this position when the United States backed away, asserting that the Committee had no more than an overseeing role. The news of this reached Buenos Aires the day before the TCDC conference ended and it was mentioned several times at the closing session, most emphatically by the Chairman of the Group of 77, Frank Francis of Jamaica. While the establishment of a new international economic order had been brought closer by the TCDC

Conference, he said, the collapse of the Committee in New York showed how much more remained to be done.

* * *

A week after the TCDC conference adjourned, the 33rd session of the U.N. General Assembly met in New York. The report of the Buenos Aires meeting was one of 129 items on the Assembly's agenda and it faced few problems in its easy passage through committee debate to plenary acceptance. On December 18, the Assembly endorsed the recommendations of the Conference and set in motion the long hard job of implementation.

11

Looking Ahead

Colonialism crippled large parts of the world materially and intellectually. It broke ancient links of trade and culture. It destroyed the independence of homegrown systems in Africa, Asia, and Latin America. It imposed with violence systems of economic exploitation and political rule which reduced great populations to poverty. All these processes of colonialism are now being reversed. A generation after World War II the entire legacy of European colonialism is under question, and much of it is in the process of being discarded. In economic terms, the central statement of intent in this regard has been the 1974 Declaration of the United Nations General Assembly on a New International Economic Order (NIEO).

It is useful to look at what has happened five years after the call for this new order. What has changed? Who did what? In that dread word of economic planners, how far has "implementation" gone?

The answers are disturbing. Much has happened—but little according to plan. The world economy has changed vastly since 1974 but it has become neither more efficient nor more just. What U.N. Secretary-General Kurt Waldheim said in 1975 is still, unfortunately, true: "The international system of economic and trade relations which was devised 30 years ago is now manifestly inadequate for the needs of the world community as a whole. The charge against that order in the past was that it worked well for the affluent and against the poor. It cannot now even be said that it works well for the affluent."

Evidence of this is hard to avoid. Over the last five years the wide range of complaints from developing countries have been joined by the loud dismay of rich countries facing double-digit inflation, rising unemployment and stagnant economies. Today, if there is wholehearted agreement on any aspect of international economics, it is on the fact that just about everyone is in serious trouble.

Why then, has there not been more and better coordinated action to create a new economic order—especially as the call for such action was made by consensus in the U.N. General Assembly?

There are two reasons. The first is that the 1974 consensus in the Assembly was only apparent, the result of an emotional confrontation between poor and rich. As U.S. Ambassador John Scali said after the resolution was adopted, it "is a significant political document, but it does not represent unanimity of opinion. To label some of these highly controversial conclusions as agreed is not only idle, it is self-deceiving." Other developed countries, in particular the members of the EEC and Japan, made similar reservations, and though their opposition since then has softened in some respects, it is undoubtedly the main reason why joint action has been painfully slow.

The other major reason for slow progress is the sheer enormity of the change proposed. Developing countries are asking nothing less than the decolonization of the world economy, their own "complete economic emancipation." This means changing economic relationships resulting from two centuries of colonialism and restructuring a system shaped for a generation after World War II by a few dominant countries. It involves changing the institutions and laws that govern the world economy, and redirecting the traffic of science, technology, money and material. It signifies a dilution of the power of the rich countries and the creation of a more democratic world. All this to be accomplished by peaceful negotiations among 150 sovereign states unequal in every economic, social, and political variable.

The whole exercise would seem unrealistic if it were not that political efforts at change are underpinned by other trends which argue forcefully for a more rational ordering of the world's economy. Population growth, the problems of food, the needs of the environment, the demand for raw materials and its supply, the development of science and technology, the maintenance of public health, the international division of labor, all are factors beyond the capacity of any country to control on its own. And they cannot be dealt with efficiently under existing global systems of cooperation. They all point to a future world where the words "self reliance" will have to go hand in hand with the apparently antithetical word "collective." As Mahmoud Mestiri, the Tunisian Ambassador to the United Nations and the current Chairman of the Group of 77 pointed out recently, "The global economy today is increasingly like the human body. It cannot be healthy in parts. If an arm or a leg, even a finger or toe, is infected, the body as a whole is in danger of infection and ill health."

This interdependence of international life was thrust upon the world's attention in 1973 by OPEC. Six years later the same message is being more gently transmitted in trade statistics showing that developing countries buy a third of the manufactured exports of developed countries. And the growing markets of the poor are ever more important for the economic health of the rich. Just how important can be gauged from current statistics that show the United States, for instance, exporting more to developing countries than to the EEC, Japan and the socialist countries combined.

But the importance of developing countries as a group in the global economy has not brought their concept of a new international order any closer. A basic tenet of that concept was coordinated and planned change that would take into consideration the interests of all countries, weak and strong. Negotiations since 1974 have sought to give life to this basic principle of equity in three ways. They have sought to forge new codes of international conduct; to create new institutions, or restructure existing ones; and to alter the actual exchanges of money, goods and ideas. The results so far have been less than stunning.

CODES OF CONDUCT

There have been three major codes of conduct upon which the world community has focused since 1974. The most comprehensive of them, and the only one adopted so far, has been the Charter of Economic Rights and Duties of States. Prepared over a 17-month period by a working group of representatives from 40 states, the charter sets standards to "protect the rights of all countries and in particular the developing states." Its 34 articles spell out the fundamental principles which should govern international economic relations.

On December 12, 1974 the U.N. General Assembly adopted the charter but there was no consensus, not even an apparent one. A roll call vote was taken and six countries voted against it: Belgium, Denmark, Federal Republic of Germany, Luxembourg, United Kingdom and the United States. Ten other developed countries abstained: Austria, Canada, France, Ireland, Israel, Italy, Japan, Netherlands, Norway and Spain. There were 120 affirmative votes.

CODE ON TECHNOLOGY

The scientific and industrial revolutions that modernized and made affluent the developed countries of today have not yet taken full effect in the poorer countries. Because of this the transfer of technology to developing countries is one of the focal points of attention in the negotiations toward a new world order. Much of the world's technology is in the hands of transnational corporations and their interests are profit, not the needs of poor societies. Often under present conditions the technology transferred to poor countries is both overpriced and inappropriate to their social and economic conditions. To deal with all these problems efforts have been underway for more than two years to create a generally applicable code of conduct.

From 1976 to 1978 a group of experts in legal, administrative and economic affairs drafted the code. In October 1978 this went to the first session of an intergovernmental negotiating conference in Geneva. During the three-week first session some progress was made, but two large questions remained unsettled: (1) Would the code have the force of law, or would it remain as a set of guidelines to be observed voluntarily? and (2) Would the scope of the code cover the extensive transfers of technology between units of transnational corporations? On both issues views were far apart.

At the beginning of the second session of the negotiating conference in February 1979 the Group of 77 expressed its dissatisfaction at the lack of progress. Manaspas Xuto of Thailand, speaking for the group, quoted from the Declaration the 77 had just adopted in Arusha: "Despite the great flexibility and political will displayed by the Group of 77 in an attempt to secure progress, it was clear that other groups lacked the political will to move forward. . . . The Group of 77 emphasizes that the progress which has been achieved had been made possible by the virtually unilateral concessions by the Group of 77."

TRANSNATIONAL CORPORATIONS

Closely allied to the question of technology is that of transnational corporations. In wealth and geographical reach, in the multiplicity of activities, in the command of resources and of power many corporations now rival nation-states. This, as well as their proclivity to pursue profit without much concern for national sensitivities has made them a subject of deep interest to governments. Work on a code of conduct for transnationals has been going on since 1977 and is scheduled to be completed in 1979.

INSTITUTIONAL CHANGE

In the jargon of international relations, "institutional change" means two things. One is the changing of the rules and regulations governing international economic relations; the other is the creation of new organizations and systems of cooperation. Into the first category fall the rules of the international monetary system embodied in the IMF, the conventions governing "intellectual property" (patents, copyrights, etc.) and the general body of regulations on trade incorporated in GATT. All these are the results of negotiation and agreement mainly among developed countries. The creation of a new world economic order implies that these sets of rules and regulations will change so as to reflect the interests of developing countries and to support their efforts at modernization and growth.

So far, the world's monetary rules and agreements on trade have changed only to the extent necessary to rescue countries in dire distress. In both areas the existing rules have been demonstrably inadequate to deal with the near chaotic developments of recent years, yet efforts to redraw them have not gone beyond the hopeful tinkering stage. As Algeria's Idriss Jazairy, 1978 Chairman of the U.N. "Committee of the Whole" on economic negotiations, pointed out, "institutional adjustment is proving to be incapable not only of guiding, but even of following the rapid chain of events on the international scene." Commenting on the same problem, IMF Managing Director J. de Larosière had this to say: "The reform of the international monetary system has been discussed for 15 years or more. It is quite clear that at the present time there is neither consensus nor any possibility for consensus to implement a new fundamental international reform . . ."

As for "intellectual property," the only international instrument governing the area, the Paris Convention for the Protection of Industrial Property, is being revised. For the first time in the history of the convention the interests of developing countries are being taken into account. A conference to adopt the changes is scheduled for 1980.

NEW STARTS

There has been slightly more progress toward the creation of new organizations and systems of cooperation. A number of new arrangements have been made at the regional and subregional levels establishing links among developing countries which had not existed before. Clearing unions, technology centers, information referral systems, news agency pools, trade protocols and a variety of other deals have surfaced over the past five years. Their impact has not been great yet, but the potential is undeniable. They are the essential foundations for cooperation and growth in the direction of a new international economic order.

At the international level, especially within the United Nations system there have been several significant developments:

- A new billion-dollar fund for agricultural development—IFAD—has gone into operation, and unlike other organizations in the U.N. system, its funds are almost equally drawn from developing and developed countries. There is also a new 36-nation World Food Council serving as the "eyes, ears and conscience" of the U.N. system on matters related to food.
- In March 1979 agreement was reached in Geneva on the basic elements of a "Common Fund" proposed by the U.N. Conference on Trade and Development (UNCTAD) to deal with the major problems of the world's commodity markets. Most developing countries are heavily dependent on exports of raw materials and basic commodities subject to wild fluctuations in price and demand in world markets. UNCTAD had proposed an

integrated program to stabilize and manage the world's commodity markets. This involved agreements between producers and consumers of a range of individual commodities, as well as a central Common Fund to finance buffer stocks and other activities. The agreement on the basic elements of the fund came after two years of intense negotiations during which the original proposals of the developing countries were considerably modified. Despite this the agreement to establish a fund is seen as an important breakthrough, for it paves the way for the creation of the first international institution in the area of world trade, an area in which the poor have been victims ever since they first fell under the domination of colonial rulers.

- In April 1979, agreement was reached on the conversion of the U.N. Industrial Development Organization (UNIDO) into a specialized agency of the U.N. system, a status that would in principle allow it greater autonomy and financial power.

ACTUAL CHANGES

Moving away from codes and frameworks, how have developing countries fared in their haggling on actual exchanges with rich countries? The answer, once again, is not positive. The Tokyo Round of negotiations under GATT, begun in 1973 and scheduled to end in July 1979, exemplifies the situation. The most comprehensive trade talks ever attempted under the auspices of GATT, the Tokyo Round is expected to aid the world's major trading nations. But it has not gone very far toward achieving the aims declared in Tokyo of helping "to secure additional benefits for the international trade of developing countries . . . achieve a substantial increase in their foreign exchange earnings, the diversification of their exports, the acceleration of the rate of growth of their trade . . . an improvement in the possibilities for these countries to participate in the expansion of world trade and a better balance as between developed and developing countries in the sharing of [resulting] advantages. . . ."

Six years after it opened, the Tokyo Round drew to its close with developing countries charging that they had been excluded from much of the negotiating. As the Malaysian representative, Yee Che Fong said, "Developing country delegations . . . had constantly pointed out the need for transparency in the negotiations. Yet today we find texts of Agreements which had been negotiated amongst a few developed countries on subjects like Trade in Civil Aircraft, of which an overwhelming majority of participants in the multilateral trade negotiations (MTN) were not aware until 7 April 1979. My country and many other developing countries are sizeable customers for civil aircraft and yet we had been kept out of the negotiations of this Agreement."

Speaking for developing countries as a group, Yugoslavia's Ambassador, Petar Tomic, sounded the same chord. But, he said, the fact that there was no "transparency" in the negotiations did not mean that "proposals and requests submitted by the developing countries were not known. It is regrettable that many of them were ignored in spite of the clearly stated objectives of the Tokyo Declaration [and of] so many resolutions, declarations and decisions taken at U.N. sessions and UNCTAD meetings." He said that there had been little progress on a number of important issues. The stated aim of achieving favorable treatment for the trade of developing countries had been largely unfulfilled and where it did exist it was poor. Work to improve the framework of international trade had been modest. The least developed countries had got little from the talks, and many opportunities to take significant steps toward a NIEO had been missed.

One particularly significant problem that Ambassador Tomic and other speakers from developing countries touched upon was that of protectionism. The "complete failure" to agree on reducing or eliminating protectionism was a matter of great regret, Ambassador Tomic said. Developed countries, particularly the members of the European Economic Community (EEC), were insisting on their rights to impose discriminatory limits on the exports of countries which proved too competitive. Such discrimination was even against GATT rules, but it was being pressed.

While the Tokyo Round was in progress a range of discriminatory arrangements had already been put into effect. As World Bank President Robert McNamara pointed out to the 1978 annual meeting of the Bank's governors, "even a partial resumé of the new restrictive measures illustrates the severity of the problem." Australia, Canada, France, the United Kingdom, the United States, and Sweden had imposed new quotas and so-called "orderly marketing arrangements" on the developing countries' exports of footwear, Mr. McNamara said. A new protocol of the Multi-Fiber Arrangement, covering the period through 1981, permitted the imposition of more severe restrictions on clothing and textiles. "Under it, for example, the European Common Market reduced 1978 quotas for three countries beneath actual 1976 levels, and severely limited the growth of quotas of other countries, including many that are only beginning to export these products."

In addition, Mr. McNamara went on, "the EEC, Australia, Canada, Norway, and Sweden also tightened developing country quotas for textiles and clothing." The United States in 1978 held three of its largest suppliers to 1977 levels. "The net effect of all of these restrictive measures will be to limit the growth of developing countries' exports of clothing and textiles to only 5 percent per annum over the next few years, compared to some 16 percent per annum in the period 1967–76," Mr. McNamara said.

Also, he went on, "The European Community and the United States have introduced special protective measures regarding steel, which pose serious difficulties for those developing countries now emerging as exporters. The United Kingdom has imposed quotas on television sets from two developing countries, and similar action is threatened in the United States and elsewhere."

As Olivier Long, the Director-General of GATT told an American audience in May 1978, such protectionist moves reflected basically "a refusal to adjust to changing competitive conditions." It was not correct "to suggest that the blame should be largely borne by the developing countries." Emotion, he said, had tended to

> obscure facts in discussion of developing country exports of manufactures. It is a fact that the flow of manufactured products from developing to developed countries has been growing faster over the last decade than the flow in the other direction.
>
> It is also a fact, however, that the balance remains overwhelmingly—in the ratio of four to one—in favor of the industrialized countries. The total value of manufactures sold by the industrialized countries to the developing countries in 1977 was about $134 billion, against purchases of only about $34 billion. For the United States alone, the ratio is two to one; for the EEC and European Free Trade Association (EFTA) countries of Western Europe, it is five to one; for Japan, it is actually ten to one. Overall, the surplus of the industrialized countries in this mutual trade in manufactures has continued, and continues, to grow.

All this happened during a period when the prices of imports from developed to developing countries boomed, while those of many of their own exports remained stagnant. As a result, UNCTAD estimates, there was a 15 percent deterioration in the terms of trade of developing countries in the period 1974 to 1978. In 1978 this signified a loss of over $30 billion in foreign exchange. Two serious consequences have been reduced development budgets and a booming external debt. The total debt burden of developing countries rose from $114 billion in 1973 to nearly $300 billion in 1978. An increasing number of countries now pay over 25 percent of their export earnings in debt-service charges. Meanwhile, the volume of official development aid has not risen in real terms since 1971.

HOPEFUL TRENDS

Despite the prevailing gloom, however, there are some signs of advance. There is, for one thing, a growing awareness in rich countries that a new world order might be in their self-interest. This is significant, even if, as India's Muchkund Dubey, chairman of the U.N. committee drawing up a strategy for the 1980s, points out, "the awareness has yet to be be translated into policy."

The swift growth in trade and other links between the socialist and market economies of the world is another development of considerable significance. The trade is fairly limited now, but is growing rapidly. UNCTAD reports that in the period 1976–1977 this rate growth (27.5 percent) has been, in fact, greater than that of trade among the socialist states themselves (24.9 percent). It is also growing faster than the trade of the socialist states with developed market economies (14.8 percent). At present only about 25 developing countries are involved in this exchange, but there is now a determined effort to increase this number. The potential for this trade is great and if realized, its implications for present economic relationships and structures would be profound.

THE U.N. SYSTEM

The events of the last five years have had a considerable impact on the U.N. system of organizations. Since 1974 every unit of the system dealing with economic and social affairs has reassessed its attitudes, examined the validity of its aims and formulated new strategies. But overall, what has been the effect? The answer was provided by U.N. Secretary-General Kurt Waldheim when he spoke to the U.N. press corps in February 1979.

The year ahead, he told them, would be "difficult. We shall be faced with many problems and unresolved issues, and the prospects for their solution are not too good. I see the situation as being rather gloomy . . . We are still faced with the same unresolved questions. . . . Regional conflicts continue. . . . There is new tension and conflict. . . . The problems of the North-South dialogue remain unresolved." Perhaps, the Secretary-General commented, the correspondents were wondering why he was so gloomy and why he was expressing his feelings so frankly. "The reason is that I am deeply concerned about the political will of the leadership in the world to solve the problems of today."

The fault was not with the machinery of the U.N. system. Mr. Waldheim explained:

> We are blamed because the governments themselves are not able to solve their problems and are not using this machinery as it should be used. Then, when a problem cannot be solved, a body, a commission or even a new organization is set up to solve it . . . if you cannot solve the North-South dialogue you restructure. I do not think the restructuring process alone can solve the problem. . . . We have to speak the truth. We have to say that we have an international instrument which is capable of making its contribution to the solution of world problems. But this instrument has to be used. If it is not, the outlook for peace will be gloomy.

While the Secretary-General was saying this in New York, the Group of 77, meeting in Arusha, Tanzania, had reached the same conclusion. Their prescription for redress was the Arusha Programme for Collective Self-Reliance and Framework for Negotiations. They decided that "during the last three years considerable progress has been made in elaborating further the details of the programme on economic cooperation among developing countries and that the technical information already available justifies the adoption of detailed operational guidelines and objectives." To this end they agreed on a range of priorities, the scope and thrust of which was summed up in the address by Tanzania's President Julius Nyerere.

> We have to build up trade among ourselves, and we have to do this quite deliberately. For it will not happen through the workings of laissez faire. We each have to search out the possibilities of purchase from other Third World nations, or sale to other Third World nations.
>
> We have to co-operate in establishing Third World Multinational Corporations, owned by us and controlled by us, to serve our purposes and to remain independent of the great transnational corporations which now dominate the world economic scene. We need Third World Shipping Lines to carry our goods, to open new links between us—and to break the strangling monopoly of the conference lines. We need Third World international insurance; it is absurd that our reinsurance premiums should provide capital for the industrialized world. We need to have institutions of research and development directed at serving our needs and developing our resources. We need to plan jointly-owned industries when our separate markets are too small for the economic viability of certain production processes. And it may be that we should be considering the idea of having our own Third World financial clearing institutions instead of paying each other through London, New York, or Paris.

The Arusha Programme covered all that and more, concentrating on the pragmatic. For, as President Nyerere pointed out, the Group of 77 had no common

> ideology. Some of us are avowedly "scientific" socialists, some just plain socialist, some capitalist, some theocratic, and some fascist! We are not necessarily friendly with each other—some countries represented here are currently engaged in a war with each other. Our national income per head varies from about $100 a year to $2,000 a year. Some of us have minerals, some do not; some of us are landlocked and others are isolated in huge oceans. The Group of 77 cannot be defined by any of these or any other economic, social, or ideological categories—membership cuts across them all.

The 77 endured as a group out of sheer necessity, Mr. Nyerere said. To attain freedom from external domination the Third World had few options: "Unity is our instrument—our only instrument."

Appendix A
Annotated List of Major Schemes and Institutions for Promoting Economic Co-operation Among Developing Countries

A. MARKET-INTEGRATION AND MARKET-SHARING SCHEMES

1. Africa

Scheme and year of establishment	Main objectives and instruments
Council of the Entente, 1959 Membership as of December 1976: Benin, Ivory Coast, Niger, Togo, Upper Volta	The general purpose is to harmonize policies. The Regional Industrialization Committee, the agricultural staples stabilization and marketing plan (both the Committee and the plan largely inactive to date), and projects in livestock, transport and communication, and training programmes have been launched.
Permanent Consultative Committee of the Maghreg, 1964 Membership as of December 1976: Algeria, Morocco, Tunisia	A draft five-year agreement on economic co-operation (not ratified) provided for partial linear reduction in customs duties and quantitative restrictions on industrial goods (with safeguard clauses); product-by-product negotiations on promoting trade in agricultural goods; and industrial co-operation arrangements. Trade among partners continues on the basis of bilateral, and, for some goods, preferential arrangements. Co-operation in other areas (e.g., transport, tourism) has been more active.

Scheme and year of establishment	Main objectives and instruments
Central African Customs and Economic Union, 1966 (Successor to the Equatorial Customs Union) Membership as of December 1976: Central African Empire, Congo, Gabon, United Republic of Cameroon	The custom union is the economic descendant of the Federation of French Equatorial Africa. The customs union incorporates a common external tariff (but allows additional national import taxes), free movement of unprocessed goods inside the area and a so-called "single tax" for processed and industrial goods intended for sale in several member States. The single tax is levied in the State where the plant is located and the proceeds are paid to the States to which deliveries are made. The union also provides for co-operation in other areas, especially transport and communications, for which a master plan for the area has been under preparation.
East African Community, 1967 (Successor to the Common Market and Common Services Organization) Membership as of December 1976: Kenya, Uganda, United Republic of Tanzania	The aim is to strengthen and regulate the industrial, commercial and other relations of the partners to promote speed and balanced development whose benefits shall be equitably shared. The means include a common external tariff; abolition of internal barriers; harmonized monetary policy, fiscal incentives and planning; a degree of freedom in mutual payments; and the joint operation of common services. The Community instruments include the "transfer-tax" system intended to promote new industries in industrially less advanced partner States; it involves temporary duties on specific manufactures produced and traded within the area which may be levied under specified conditions by countries in deficit in manufactured goods trade within the Community. As of 1977 the Community as an entity had become *de facto* inoperative.
Union of Central African States, 1968 Membership as of December 1976: Chad, Zaire	The original agreement provides for an elimination of import and export duties on mutual trade, the adoption of a common external tariff, freedom of movement for people, services and capital, the establishment of various institutions and mechanisms for harmonious development. Lack of contiguity and expensive transport costs have tended to limit the potential for co-operation.
West African Economic Community, 1973 (Successor to West African Customs and Economic Union) Membership as of December 1976: Ivory Coast, Mali, Mauritania, Niger, Senegal, Upper Volta	The aims are threefold: to promote industrialization by maintaining an economic equilibrium among the members; to improve the infrastructure related to trade, transport and communications; and to promote trade within the area. As to the latter the specific aim is to have free-trade in non-industrial products, a preference scheme for industrial products, and a common external

Scheme and year of establishment	Main objectives and instruments
	tariff. The industrial preference scheme is based on a system which replaces import duties on goods from within the Community by a lower regional co-operation tax levied on similar imported or locally made goods. The tax finances the Community Development Fund (set up in 1976) which in turn compensates countries for loss of customs revenue due to removal of import duties.
Mano River Union, 1973 Membership as of December 1976: Liberia, Sierra Leone	The aim is to expand mutual trade by eliminating trade barriers, and generally to promote the development of the two countries. A customs union is to be achieved in two stages. The first stage, to be activated during 1977, involves the liberalization of trade in goods of local origin, and the harmonization of import duties as well as of incentives to local production, and the development of instruments of co-operation for promoting production in agriculture and industry.
Economic Community of West African States, 1975 Membership as of December 1976: Benin, Chad, Gambia, Guinea, Guinea-Bissau, Ivory Coast, Liberia, Mali, Mauritania, Niger, Nigeria, Senegal, Sierra Leone, Togo, Upper Volta	The aim is to create a customs union over a 15-year period, and to harmonize industrial and agricultural policies. The agreement also provides for the eventual free movement of labour and capital and the setting up of joint enterprises.
Economic Community of the Great Lake Countries, 1976 Membership as of December 1976: Burundi, Rwanda, Zaire	The aim is increased co-operation, including trade liberalization. Specific measures are being explored following the signing of the convention establishing the Community.

2. Asia[a]

Regional Co-operation for Development, 1964 Membership as of June 1977: Iran, Pakistan, Turkey	The goals of the scheme encompass a wide range of activities: freer movement of goods between the countries; closer co-operation between their Chambers of Commerce; formulation of joint projects; reduction in postal rates; improvement in regional air service, eventual establishment of a joint airline; co-operation in other areas of infrastructure, including shipping, road and rail

[a]Including some schemes to which not only Asian but also some African countries belong.

Scheme and year of establishment

Main objectives and instruments

links; joint promotion of tourism; and the provision of technical assistance to each other. Cooperation has been achieved in numerous fields including a trade agreement, signed in 1968. In 1967 members signed an agreement on multilateral payments arrangements to facilitate their trade. An original form of industrial co-operation has been undertaken: the joint-purpose enterprise. These have been set up based either on participation of the three in equity capital or on commitments to buy output. A treaty was signed in March 1977 to establish a free trade area over a 10-year period by eliminating tariff and non-tariff barriers and by promoting regional projects.

Association of South East Asian Nations, 1967

Membership as of June 1977: Indonesia, Malaysia, Philippines, Singapore, Thailand

The goals are economic, social and cultural development of the subregion; promotion of peace and stability in area; encouragement of co-operation and mutual assistance in areas of common interest, including the educational, technical, scientific, and administrative fields; co-operation to develop agriculture, industry, transport and communications, expand trade, and raise the level of living of the inhabitants of the subregion; co-operation as a unit with other organizations. An agreement, in principle, was reached in 1975 on a gradual reduction of mutual trade barriers and eventual creation of a free-trade area. A 10 per cent cut in tariffs on reciprocal trade was agreed to in February 1977. The first industry-sharing package was decided in March 1977.

Arab Common Market, 1971

Membership as of June 1977: Egypt, Iraq, Jordan, Sudan, Syrian Arab Republic

A subdivision of the Agreement on Arab Economic Unity—comprising Democratic Yemen, Egypt, Iraq, Jordan, Kuwait, Libyan Arab Jamahiriya, Mauritania, Somalia, Sudan, Syrian Arab Republic, United Arab Emirates, Yemen—which entered into force in 1964. The goal of this Agreement is the gradual achievement among the parties of full economic unity as characterized by freedom of movement of people, goods and capital; freedom of residence, work, employment and exercise of economic activity, as well as freedom of transport and transit. Only five of the parties to the Agreement have taken the necessary steps to form a free-trade area and together they constitute the so-called Arab Common Market. Their goal has been the creation of a free-trade area through the abolition of any remaining tariff barriers and quantitative restrictions on

Scheme and year of establishment	Main objectives and instruments

mutual trade in all goods with the exception of tobacco. Egypt, Iraq, Jordan and the Syrian Arab Republic—Sudan became a member in May 1977—abolished tariffs on imports of manufactures from each other in 1973. A common external tariff is to be introduced gradually in the period 1978–1981.

3. Latin America and the Caribbean

Latin American Free Trade Association, 1960

Membership as of December 1976: Argentina, Bolivia, Brazil, Chile, Colombia, Mexico, Paraguay, Peru, Uruguay, Venezuela

The aim is to create a free-trade area through trade liberalization. Three main mechanisms: (a) national lists of products on which each country grants gradual tariff reductions to all others; (b) common list of items on which contracting parties agree to reduce tariff and non-tariff restrictions; (c) complementarity agreements. Common external tariff is a long-term objective. Special list of non-extensive tariff concessions in favour of less industrialized countries. Free trade originally expected to be achieved by 1973. However, tariff reductions and lessening of other import restrictions have fallen well behind schedule.

Central American Common Market, 1960

Membership as of December 1976: Costa Rica, El Salvador, Guatemala, Honduras, Nicaragua

The aim is to create a free trade area and customs union. Mechanisms: tariff liberalization, unification of external tariffs, establishment of financial institutions, special régime for some industries, infrastructure development. By 1968, all but 21 items liberalized, and unified external tariff on all but 37 items. Suspension of free trade by Honduras in 1970. At present, complete restructuring of the system is being considered.

Andean Group, 1968

Membership as of December 1976: Bolivia, Colombia, Ecuador, Peru, Venezuela

The aim is to promote harmonious development of member countries through market integration and joint programming. Mechanisms: reduction of tariffs with special régimes for products subject to industrial programming; unification of external tariffs; joint industrial programming; harmonization of exchange, monetary, financial and fiscal policies. Special treatment for less industrialized member countries. Notwithstanding significant advances in market integration and approval of two sector industrial development programmes, Chile withdrew in 1976, and this has led to certain readjustments.

Scheme and year of establishment	Main objectives and instruments
Caribbean Community, 1973 (Successor to Caribbean Free Trade Association established in 1968) Membership as of December 1976: Barbados, Belize, Guyana, Jamaica, Trinidad and Tobago and the members of the East Caribbean Common Market: Antigua, Dominica, Grenada, Montserrat, St. Kitts-Nevis-Anguilla, St. Lucia, St. Vincent	The goals are economic integration through the establishment of a Common Market, collaboration for provision of common services (shipping, air transport, industrial research, health education), and co-ordination of foreign policies. Main instruments: liberalization of imports of products originating in the subregion (with certain exceptions) by reducing tariffs and eliminating other restrictions, common external tariff, import substitution of agricultural products on a sub-regional basis, co-ordinated industrial promotion, and centralized negotiations on transport undertakings and transport tariffs. Special treatment for less industrialized countries in the area, regarding liberalization schedule and promotion of industrial development.
Latin American Economic System, 1975 Membership as of December 1976: Argentina, Bolivia, Brazil, Chile, Colombia, Costa Rica, Cuba, Dominican Republic, Ecuador, El Salvador, Grenada, Guatemala, Guyana, Haiti, Honduras, Jamaica, Mexico, Nicaragua, Panama, Paraguay, Peru, Trinidad and Tobago, Uruguay, Venezuela	The main objectives are (a) promotion of intraregional co-operation to achieve self-sustaining and independent development in the region, and (b) permanent consultation and co-ordination to agree on common strategies regarding economic and social development and to formulate common positions vis-à-vis third countries. Mechanisms: promotion of multinational enterprises among member countries; special stimulus to agriculture, energy and basic industrial goods; increased processing of raw materials, industrial complementation and exports of manufactures; strengthening of bargaining position of the region; co-operation on development of technology; development of transport and tourism, particularly in an intraregional context; support of market integration schemes; exchange of information regarding transnationals; special treatment to less developed, land-locked and small-size member countries.

B. DEVELOPMENT-FINANCING INSTITUTIONS

1. Regional development banks and subregional financial institutions

(a) AFRICA

Institution and year of establishment	Main objectives and level of operations
African Development Bank, 1964 (first loan made in 1967) Membership as of December 1976: Algeria, Benin, Botswana, Burundi, Central African Empire, Chad, Congo, Egypt, Equatorial Guinea, Ethiopia, Gabon, Gambia, Ghana, Guinea, Guinea-Bissau, Ivory Coast, Kenya, Lesotho, Liberia, Libyan Arab Jamahiriya, Malawi, Mali, Mauritania, Mauritius, Morocco, Niger, Nigeria, Rwanda, Senegal, Sierra Leone, Somalia, Sudan, Swaziland, Togo, Tunisia, Uganda, United Republic of Tanzania, Upper Volta, Zaire, Zambia Membership of the Fund (soft loan facility of the Bank) also includes several non-regional developing country members— Argentina, Brazil and Saudi Arabia—as well as Belgium, Canada, Denmark, Finland, Germany, Federal Republic of, Italy, Japan, Norway, Netherlands, Spain, Sweden, Switzerland, United Kingdom, and Yugoslavia	The aim is to help the development and integration of African countries, principally by financing projects of common interest, such as multinational ventures or projects to enhance the complementarity of the different economies. Other instruments include the promotion of foreign investment in the region, the mobilization of resources, the studying and preparation of projects, and the provision of technical assistance in the study, preparation and execution projects. The Bank also administers some funds to help African petroleum-importing countries, and has set up the International Financial Corporation for Investment and Development in Africa (based in Geneva) which attracts private investment into Africa ($12.7 million as of 1976). Total loans and grants by the Bank up to the end of 1975 amounted to $405 million in commitments and $108 million in disbursements.
East African Development Bank, 1967 Membership as of December 1976: Kenya, Uganda, United Republic of Tanzania (as well as African Development Bank and several commercial institutions operating in the community)	The aims of the Bank are to promote balanced industrial development in the community in such a way that the less advanced industrial partners are given greater stimulus and that the industries of the three partner countries can become more complementary. The Bank's resources are derived from its subscribed capital, as well as loans and credits from both international and national (official or commercial) organizations. By the

Institution and year of establishment	Main objectives and level of operations
	end of 1973 loan approvals totalled 245 million Units of Account, and disbursements about 130 million Units of Account (one Unit being equivalent to one Uganda shilling, or 0.14 United States dollars at the beginning of 1973).

The Mutual Aid and Loan Guaranty Fund of the Council of the Entente States, 1973 (Successor to earlier Fund set up in 1966 and to Solidarity Fund in 1959)

Membership as of December 1976: Benin, Ivory Coast, Niger, Togo, and Upper Volta

The aims of the Fund are, first, to guarantee loans of member States, public or semi-public bodies and certain private enterprises, second, to finance viable projects in agriculture, commerce and industry and infrastructure, and, third, to promote development by other means, including the co-ordination of efforts in tackling problems whose solution requires common action by the countries of the area. The Fund's resources are derived mainly from annual member contributions (totalling 5.3 billion CFA francs at the end of 1974, and planned to increase to 8.5 billion over the next five years), as well as grants, proceeds of investments and fees for its services.

West African Development Bank, 1974

Signatories were members of the Central Bank and Monetary Union of West African States (Benin, Ivory Coast, Niger, Senegal, Togo and Upper Volta) and open to other West African States

The aim is balanced development and integration of West Africa, particularly its member States. The Bank is intended to promote and finance development projects, encourage the transfer of enterprises into local ownership, help to attract outside capital and encourage the pooling of internally available resources. The initial capital was set at 214 billion CFA francs, divided equally into contributions from the respective Governments on the one hand, and the Central Bank of West African States on the other.

Fund for Co-operation, Compensation and Developmnent of the Economic Community of West African States, 1975

Membership as of December 1976: Benin, Gambia, Ghana, Guinea, Guinea-Bissau, Ivory Coast, Liberia, Mali, Mauritania, Niger, Nigeria, Senegal, Sierra Leone, Togo and Upper Volta

The purpose of the Fund is to finance projects within the Community, guarantee foreign investments in designated industrial enterprises, help with the implementation of projects in less developed Community States, and offer compensation to countries sustained as a result of trade liberalization or the location of ECOWAS enterprises. The resources of the Fund are to be derived from member contributions and the income deriving from ECOWAS enterprises.

Development Bank of the Central African States, to be established

Draft convention was approved in 1975 by representatives of member countries of the Bank of

The Bank would finance development projects in the subregion. According to the draft convention establishing the Bank, the initial capital would be 16 billion CFA francs.

Institution and year of establishment	Main objectives and level of operations

Central African States (Central African Empire, Chad, Congo, Gabon, United Republic of Cameroon)

(b) ASIA

Asian Development Bank, 1966

Membership as of December 1976 includes Afghanistan, Australia, Bangladesh, Burma, Cook Islands, Democratic Kampuchea, Fiji, Gilbert Islands, Hong Kong, India, Indonesia, Japan, Lao People's Democratic Republic, Malaysia, Nepal, New Zealand, Pakistan, Papua New Guinea, Philippines, Republic of Korea, Singapore, Socialist Republic of Viet Nam, Solomon Islands, Sri Lanka, Thailand, Tongo, Western Samoa and (non-regional members) Austria, Belgium, Canada, Denmark, Finland, France, Germany (Federal Republic of), Italy, Netherlands, Norway, Sweden, Switzerland, United Kingdom of Great Britain and Northern Ireland and the United States of America

The purpose of the Bank is to foster economic growth and co-operation in the region, with special regard to be given to the needs of the smaller or less developed member countries in the region. The Bank can lend to any member and private or public enterprise operating in a member's country, and to any regional or other international agency concerned with the region's development. It may make equity investments and guarantee loans in which it participates. It also provides technical assistance. Total loans approved until 30 September 1976: $3,009 million (in 1975: $660 million).

Association of South East Asian Nations Fund, 1969

Membership as of June 1977: Indonesia, Malaysia, Philippines, Singapore, Thailand

The purpose of the Fund is to finance joint projects in member countries. The Fund is formed by five nationally held funds initially endowed with $1 million each.

(c) LATIN AMERICA AND THE CARIBBEAN

Inter-American Development Bank, 1959

Membership as of March 1977: Argentina, Austria, Barbados, Belgium, Bolivia, Brazil, Canada, Chile, Colombia, Costa Rica, Denmark, Dominican

The aim is to speed up the economic development of member developing countries, individually and collectively, through loans for financing development projects and provision of technical assistance and advice in project identification and evaluation. Credits granted until December 1976 to support economic integration

Institution and year of establishment	Main objectives and level of operations
Republic, Ecuador, El Salvador, France, Germany, Federal Republic of, Guatemala, Guyana, Haiti, Honduras, Israel, Jamaica, Japan, Mexico, Netherlands, Nicaragua, Panama, Paraguay, Peru, Spain, Switzerland, Trinidad and Tobago, United Kingdom, United States of America, Uruguay, Venezuela, Yugoslavia	(export financing and regional projects and studies) amounted to $1.4 billion. Total disbursements and total commitments amounted to $5,783 million and $10,222 million, respectively, in the period 1961–1976. Loans approved in 1976 reached $1,528 million.
Central American Bank for Economic Integration, 1960 Membership as of December 1976: Costa Rica, El Salvador, Guatemala, Honduras, Nicaragua	The aim is to promote economic integration through development loans, equity investments and provision of technical assistance. Loan activities cover agriculture, industry, infrastructure and export financing. With the exception of housing, the Bank is precluded from financing projects which are essentially local or national in scope. Total loans granted until June 1976: $759 million. Loan operations in 1975/76 amounted to $138 million.
Andean Development Corporation, 1968 Membership as of June 1977: Bolivia, Colombia, Ecuador, Peru, Venezuela	The aim is to promote economic integration among member countries through investments in projects of common interest, assistance in pre-investment studies and credits to finance exports to other members. Particular emphasis on development of joint manufacturing ventures among member countries and on projects in the less industrialized among them. Total operations approved until December 1976: $236 million. Total operations approved in 1976 amounted to $71 million.
Caribbean Development Bank, 1970 Membership as of December 1976: Antigua, Bahamas, Barbados, Belize, British Virgin Islands, Cayman Islands, Montserrat, Turks and Caicos Islands, Dominica, Grenada, Guyana, Jamaica, St. Kitts-Nevis-Anguilla, St. Lucia, St. Vincent, Trinidad and Tobago, and—four contributing members not	The aims are to promote harmonious development of the member countries in the Caribbean and to foster economic co-operation and integration among them. Special regard to the needs of less developed members. The Bank finances projects and programmes of regional members, stimulates the development of capital markets within the region and promotes identification and preparation of projects. Loans authorized until December 1976: $115 million.

Institution and year of establishment	Main objectives and level of operations

eligible to borrow—Canada, Colombia, the United Kingdom and Venezuela

Caribbean Investment Corporation, 1973

Membership as of December 1976: Antigua, Barbados, Belize, Dominica, Grenada, Guyana, Jamaica, Montserrat, St. Kitts-Nevis-Anguilla, St. Lucia, St. Vincent, Trinidad and Tobago

The aim is to foster industrial development of less developed countries in CARICOM through equity investments, guarantee of suppliers' credits, support of pre-feasibility studies and provision of technical assistance. Authorized capital as of December 1975: $7.5 million (60 per cent Governments' holding of the equity and the private sector 40 per cent). Total operations approved until 1975 amounted to nearly $1 million.

Trust Fund for the Development of the River Plate Basin, 1974

Membership as of December 1976: Argentina, Bolivia, Brazil, Paraguay, Uruguay

The aims are to promote harmonious development and physical integration of the River Plate Basin by providing financial support to relevant studies, projects and programmes. The Fund can negotiate loans, guarantees and endorsements. Authorized capital as of December 1976: $100 million.

2. Interregional development banks and funds

(a) MULTINATIONAL INSTITUTIONS

Arab Fund for Economic Social Development, 1968

Membership as of December 1974: Algeria, Bahrain, Democratic Yemen, Egypt, Iraq, Jordan, Kuwait, Lebanon, Libyan Arab Jamahiriya, Mauritania, Morocco, Oman, Qatar, Saudi Arabia, Somalia, Sudan, Syrian Arab Republic, Tunisia, United Arab Emirates, Yemen

The Fund provides finance for development projects in Arab countries by means of loans granted on easy terms to Governments and public or private institutions for projects vital to the region or for joint projects among Arab countries; encourages the investment of public and private capital; promotes the development of the regional Arab economy; and provides technical assistance. Agreement establishing the Fund fixed its subscribed capital at $342 million, which was raised to $1.4 billion in 1975. The Fund commitments were $194 million in 1975 and $128 million in the first half of 1976. The grant element of commitments is in the range of 37 to 42 percent for least developed recipients and 22 to 26 percent for other borrowers.

Inter-Arab Investment Guarantee Corporation, 1970

The Corporation provides insurance coverage for Arab investors through compensation for losses

Institution and year of establishment	**Main objectives and level of operations**

Membership as of January 1975: Algeria, Egypt, Iraq, Jordan, Kuwait, Lebanon, Libyan Arab Jamahiriya, Morocco, Mauritania, Qatar, Sudan, Syrian Arab Republic, Tunisia, United Arab Emirates, Yemen

resulting from certain events with the goal of encouraging the flow of private capital between Arab countries. The agreement establishing the Corporation specified that it must provide total or partial coverage for losses stemming from non-commercial risks (the results, for example, of nationalization, seizure, expropriation, the introduction of new regulations limiting capital repatriation or profit transfers, military action, revolutions or coup d'etats). The initial agreement established a capitalization of $34.2 million. The paid-in capital as of 31 July 1975 stood at $5.13 million.

Islamic Development Bank, 1974

Membership as of June 1975: Afghanistan, Algeria, Bahrain, Bangladesh, Chad, Egypt, Guinea, Indonesia, Jordan, Kuwait, Lebanon, Libyan Arab Jamahiriya, Malaysia, Mali, Mauritania, Morocco, Niger, Oman, Pakistan, Qatar, Saudi Arabia, Senegal, Somalia, Sudan, Syrian Arab Republic, Tunisia, Turkey, United Arab Emirates, United Republic of Cameroon, Yemen

The Bank mobilizes resources to finance the economic and social development of its member countries and Muslim communities. To this end it will participate in the equity capital of enterprises set up in member States, invest in economic and social infrastructure projects, make loans to the public and private sectors, establish and operate special funds for specific purposes, assist in the promotion of trade and provide technical assistance. The agreement establishing the Bank fixed its authorized capital at $2,309 million. The subscribed capital in February 1976 amounted to $874 million and the paid-in capital to $173 million.

Arab Petroleum Investment Company, 1974

Membership as of July 1974: Algeria, Bahrain, Egypt, Iraq, Kuwait, Libyan Arab Jamahiriya, Qatar, Saudi Arabia, Syrian Arab Republic, United Arab Emirates

The Company assists with the financing and capitalization of petroleum industries and ancillary industrial projects and services, the first priority being given to projects jointly undertaken by member countries. Its activities include the study and preparation of projects for investment; direct investment in the petroleum sector; the acquisition of portfolio investments; the provision of medium- and long-term loans to finance investments in petroleum industries; underwriting and the guaranteeing of securities of companies operating in member States and guaranteeing the repayment of loans provided by other financial institutions. The agreement establishing the Company fixed its authorized capital at $1,026 million. As of June 1975, its subscribed capital stood at $342 million, its paid-in capital at $171 million.

Institution and year of establishment	Main objectives and level of operations
Special Arab Fund for Africa, 1974 Membership as of October 1974: Algeria, Iraq, Kuwait, Libyan Arab Jamahiriya, Oman, Qatar, Saudi Arabia, United Arab Emirates	The Fund provides soft loans to African countries; Arab countries are, however, excluded from being possible recipients on the ground that other resources are available to them. The Arab Bank for Economic Development in Africa is charged with its administration. As of December 1975, contributions to the Fund amounted to $185 million; disbursements totalled roughly $150 million to 28 countries (selected according to such criteria as the proportion of imported petroleum to total imports, *per capita* income, the existence of drought or famine conditions, the existence of trade and payments deficits, or the availability of raw materials and energy sources).
Arab Bank for Investment and Foreign Trade, 1974 Signatories in April 1974: Algeria, Libyan Arab Jamahiriya, United Arab Emirates	The Algerian Foreign Bank, the Libyan Arab Bank and the United Arab Emirates signed the agreement by which the Bank is to undertake all operations normally performed by commercial banks in addition to making short-, medium-, and long-term investments and financing foreign trade. The main goal, however, is the mobilization of resources for investment purposes in the Arab countries and Africa. The agreement establishing the Bank set its authorized capital at the equivalent of approximately $15 million, which is fully subscribed. As of early 1977, the paid-in capital stood at $7.5 million.
Arab Bank for Economic Development in Africa, 1974 Membership as of May 1976: Algeria, Bahrain, Egypt, Iraq, Jordan, Kuwait, Lebanon, Libyan Arab Jamahiriya, Mauritania, Morocco, Oman, Palestine Liberation Organization, Qatar, Saudi Arabia, Sudan, Syrian Arab Republic, Tunisia, United Arab Emirates	While the Bank was set up to give financial assistance to African countries not belonging to the Arab League, only Arab countries can be members. The Bank's goals are to collaborate in the economic development of African countries, to encourage the use of Arab capital from outside sources for their development and to provide necessary technical assistance. To this end, it will provide loans to national and regional development finance institutions, finance the foreign exchange component of important agricultural and industrial projects, provide technical and financial aid in identifying economic development projects and acquiring technological know-how. The authorized capital of $231 million was fully subscribed as of May 1976. Twelve loans totalling $86 million were approved in November 1975 and nine more, totalling $58 million, in the first half of 1976. The grant element of these loans ranged from 28 to 57 per cent.

Institution and year of establishment	Main objectives and level of operations
Arab Investment Company, 1974 Membership as of May 1976: Abu Dhabi, Bahrain, Egypt, Iraq, Jordan, Kuwait, Morocco, Qatar, Saudi Arabia, Sudan, Syrian Arab Republic, Tunisia	The Company promotes investment of Arab capital in the economic development of the member States by carrying out projects in the areas of agriculture, industry, commerce and services. The authorized capital: $225 million. As of May 1976, the paid-in capital stood at $240 million. By 31 July 1975, authorized investments amounted to $32 million.
Arab Fund for Technical Assistance to Arab and African Countries, 1974 Membership as of May 1976: Algeria, Egypt, Iraq, Morocco, Libyan Arab Republic, Palestine Liberation Organization, Qatar, Saudi Arabia, Sudan, Tunisia, United Arab Emirates, Yemen	The Fund co-ordinates and finances technical-assistance programmes arranged by the League of Arab States and Arab specialized agencies; prepares surveys of development projects in Arab and African countries; provides consultancy services and experts and organizes their exchange between Arab and African countries; and co-ordinates scientific and technological development between these countries. The Sixth Arab Summit fixed the Fund's capital at $15 million in 1974. This was raised to $25 million by the Seventh Summit. The Fund began operation in May 1975.
Organization of Arab Petroleum Exporting Countries, Special Account, 1974 Membership as of June 1974: Algeria, Bahrain, Egypt, Iraq, Kuwait, Libyan Arab Jamahiriya, United Arab Emirates	The OAPEC Special Account emergency assistance to the poorest Arab countries in the form of untied interest-free loans with 20 years maturity and a 10-year grace period. The amount pledged in the first instance was nearly $80 million which it was agreed to distribute as follows: Democratic Yemen, 14.1 per cent; Mauritius, 5.9 per cent; Morocco, 10.2 per cent; Somalia, 9.1 per cent; Sudan, 46.9 per cent; and Yemen, 13.8 per cent. The Council of Ministers of OAPEC agreed to renew the Special Account for 1975, and in May of that year OAPEC members, with the exception of Iraq, replenished the Special Account.
OPEC Special Fund, 1976 Membership as of January 1976: Algeria, Ecuador, Gabon, Indonesia, Iran, Iraq, Kuwait, Libyan Arab Jamahiriya, Nigeria, Qatar, Saudi Arabia, United Arab Emirates, Venezuela	The Fund expends long-term, interest-free loans for balance-of-payments support and for the financing of development projects and programmes in developing countries, without geographical or political restrictions. Its initial capitalization was $800 million. The initial agreement stipulated one-year life span for the Fund. The aim is to operate with minimum of new administrative machinery but with maximum collaboration with existing aid-giving bodies in member States.

Institution and year of establishment	Main objectives and level of operations
Arab Authority for Agricultural Investment and Development, 1976 Membership as of April 1976: Algeria, Egypt, Iraq, Kuwait, Libyan Arab Jamahiriya, Mauritania, Morocco, Qatar, Saudi Arabia, Somalia, Sudan, Syrian Arab Republic, United Arab Emirates	The Authority provides investment and development resources in an integrated programme specifically formulated to achieve predetermined production targets within an over-all framework of national development objectives. The initial capitalization, especially set with the requirements of the Authority's first undertaking—the First Investment Plan of the Basic Programme for Agricultural Development in the Democratic Republic of the Sudan—in mind, is approximately $517 million, of which nearly $400 million had been subscribed by October 1976.
Gulf Authority for the Development of Egypt, 1976 Membership as of October 1976: Egypt, Kuwait, Qatar, Saudi Arabia, United Arab Emirates	Established with a capitalization of $2,000 million, the Gulf Authority is unique among the Arab funds in that it was formed with the primary intention of assisting one particular State through its present economic and financial difficulties. Egypt's original goal was the creation of a larger assistance fund to support its 1976–1980 Five-Year Plan, with the proviso that part of the allocated funds could also be utilized for budgetary and balance-of-payments support. The four donors reformulated objectives and it was therefore agreed that the Authority would, first, provide project finance and, second, engage in activities designed to offset Egypt's balance-of-payments deficit.

(b) BILATERAL INSTITUTIONS

Kuwait Fund for Arab Economic Development, 1961	The Fund was set up as the main arm of the Government of Kuwait for the provision of loans and technical assistance to Arab countries for the implementation of their development programmes. The initital capitalization was $141 million, which was raised to $3,400 million in 1974, when its mandate was extended from solely Arab States to all developing countries. The Fund has no preference regarding national, bilateral or multinational projects and no sectoral limits are imposed although it has shown a preference for infrastructures, basic industries and the exploitation of natural resources, in that order.
Abu Dhabi Fund for Arab Economic Development, 1971	Established as an arm of the Government of Abu Dhabi to help Arab countries in their economic development through the provision of loans or

Institution and year of establishment	Main objectives and level of operations

participation in projects. The initial capitalization was $105 million, which was increased to $500 million in 1974. The Fund does not distinguish between developing countries in the granting of loans, does not provide programme loans, has no preference between national and multinational projects and has no *a priori* preference as regards sector. Its total loan commitments at the end of June 1975 stood at $215 million, equity participation at $6 million and technical assistance grants at $16 million.

The Libyan Arab Foreign Bank, 1972

The Bank, government-owned, was set up with a capitalization of $61 million to undertake normal banking operations and development financing activities outside the Libyan Arab Jamahiriya. It has provided non-concessional development loans to Algeria, Egypt, Tunisia, Uganda and Zaire and has been active in participating in joint ventures in other developing countries (for instance, setting up joint banks in Abu Dhabi, Chad, Lebanon, Mauritania, Spain, Tunisia and Uganda).

The Iraqi Fund for Foreign Development, 1974

The Fund was established to promote the economic integration and development of Arab countries as well as the economic and social development of other developing nations. It provides medium- and long-term concessional loans, participates in development projects, encourages the investment of public and private capital, offers technical assistance and finances prefeasibility and feasibility studies. The Fund's capitalization is $169 million.

Saudi Fund for Development, 1974

Established with a capital of $2,840 million, the Fund began operation in April 1975, its main purpose being to act as a government agency entrusted with the provision of project lending to developing countries, mainly in the fields of infrastructure and agriculture. Between April and July 1975, the Fund committed roughly $470 million to projects in Egypt, Indonesia, Malaysia, Mali, Sudan, Tunisia and Uganda.

The Venezuelan Investment Fund, 1974

Established by the Government of Venezuela as an instrument to make efficient use of increased revenues from petroleum. Of a capital amounting to $6,300 million, the Fund is authorized to channel 15 per cent of its resources to financial

Institution and year of establishment	Main objectives and level of operations
	co-operation. From it, two main schemes have been instituted in 1975: (a) the Venezuelan Trust Fund with $500 million to be administered by the Inter-American Development Bank; and (b) the special credit line to finance projects and development programmes in Costa Rica, El Salvador, Guatemala, Honduras, Nicaragua and Panama with scheduled annual disbursements of nearly $80 million for the period 1975–1980.

Appendix B:
The Buenos Aires Plan of Action

I. INTRODUCTION

1. The United Nations Conference on Technical Co-operation among Developing Countries comes to a critical point in the evolution of relations among developing countries themselves and between them and developed countries.

2. Profound changes are taking place in international political and economic relationships. When the principal institutions of the present international system were first established, a group of industrialized countries were dominant in world affairs. However, the historic process of decolonization now makes it possible for a large number of States, representing an overwhelming proportion of the world's population, to participate in international affairs. Moreover, substantial changes are taking place at the world level in the control and distribution of resources and in the capabilities and needs of nations. As a result of these changes and other international developments, the expansion of international relations and co-operation and the interdependence of nations are progressively increasing. Interdependence, however, demands sovereign and equal participation in the conduct of international relations and the equitable distribution of benefits.

3. The international system is in a state of ferment. Concepts, political and economic positions, institutions and relationships must be adjusted to the new realities and changing perceptions. It is in this perspective that the countries of the developing world have made their call for the new international economic order as an expression of their political will and their determination, based on the principles of national and collective self-reliance, to work towards a new pattern of international relations more appropriate to the real circumstances and reflecting fully the interests of the world community as a whole.

4. There is a growing recognition of the urgency and magnitude of the problems that are being faced and will increasingly be faced by the world community in the future. The problems of development—social and economic, national and international—demand greatly increased, concerted efforts by the developing and developed countries if the new international economic order is to be a reality. While the progress of the developing countries depends primarily on their own efforts, that progress is also affected by the policies and performance of the developed countries. At the same time it is evident that, as a consequence of widening international relations, co-operation and interdependence in many fields, the progress of the developed countries is now, and will increasingly be, affected by the policies and performance of the developing countries.

5. In this historic new stage of progress towards the attainment of the new international economic order, technical co-operation among developing countries (TCDC) is becoming a critically important dimension. It is a means of building communication and of promoting wider and more effective co-operation among developing countries. It is a vital force for

initiating, designing, organizing and promoting co-operation among developing countries so that they can create, acquire, adapt, transfer and pool knowledge and experience for their mutual benefit and for achieving national and collective self-reliance, which are essential for their social and economic development.

6. This form of co-operation is not new. A large number of co-operative activities have been carried out among developing countries over the years and many are now in progress. What is new, however, is that co-operation among developing countries is now perceived by those countries to be increasingly important in promoting sound development in the present world context. Furthermore, the difficulties currently encountered by the world economy make it even more necessary for the developing countries to evolve strategies based on greater national and collective self-reliance, for which TCDC is an important instrument. This in no way reduces the responsibility of developed countries to undertake the necessary policy measures, in particular the increase of development assistance for accelerated development of developing countries.

7. TCDC is a multidimensional process. It can be bilateral or multilateral in scope, and subregional, regional or interregional in character. It should be organized by and between Governments which can promote, for this purpose, the participation of public organizations and, within the framework of the policies laid down by Governments, that of private organizations and individuals. It may rely on innovative approaches, methods and techniques particularly adapted to local needs and, at the same time, use existing modalities of technical co-operation to the extent that these are useful. While the main flows of technical co-operation visualized would be between two or more developing countries, the support of developed countries and of regional and interregional institutions may be necessary.

8. TCDC is neither an end in itself nor a substitute for technical co-operation with developed countries. Increased technical co-operation of the developed countries is required for the transfer of appropriate technologies and also for the transfer of advanced technologies and other expertise in which they have manifest advantages. Further contributions from the developed countries are required for the enhancement of technological capabilities of developing countries through support to relevant institutions in those countries. TCDC can serve the purpose of increasing the capacity of developing countries to adapt and absorb appropriate inputs from developed countries.

9. The importance of co-operation among developing countries in general, and of technical co-operation in particular, has been recognized in a series of declarations, resolutions and decisions of the United Nations General Assembly and other bodies. In its most recent resolution on the Conference (resolution 32/183 of 19 December 1977), the General Assembly, recalling its earlier resolutions 3201 (S-VI) and 3202 (S-VI) of 1 May 1974 containing the Declaration and the Programme of Action on the establishment of a New International Economic Order, 3281 (XXIX) of 12 December 1974 containing the Charter of Economic Rights and Duties of States and 3362 (S-VII) of 16 September 1975 on development and international economic co-operation, recognized that the basic objectives of technical co-operation among developing countries were the furthering of the national and collective self-reliance of developing countries and the enhancement of their creative capacity to solve their development problems. The same objectives, within a broader context, had been strongly supported at the Fifth Conference of Heads of State or Government of Non-Aligned Countries, held at Colombo from 16 to 19 August 1976;[1] at the Conference on Economic Co-operation among Developing Countries, held at Mexico City from 13 to 22 September 1976;[2] by the Cairo Declaration of March 1977 on Afro-Arab Co-operation;[3] at the First Conference

---

[1] See A/31/197.
[2] See A/C.2/31/7 and Addendum 1.
[3] See A/32/61.

of Ministers of Labour of the non-aligned and other developing countries, held at Tunis from 24 to 26 April 1978, which adopted a programme of action and co-operation in the spheres of employment and the development of human resources;[4] and most recently by the Declaration and Action Programme for Economic Co-operation adopted by the Conference of Foreign Ministers of Non-Aligned countries held at Belgrade in July 1978.[5]

10. The General Assembly, by its resolution 32/182 of 19 December 1977, endorsed the recommendations of the Working Group on Technical Co-operation among Developing Countries,[6] as modified by the relevant decisions on technical co-operation among developing countries adopted at the eighteenth, twenty-third and twenty-fourth sessions of the Governing Council of the United Nations Development Programme, thus recognizing that those recommendations represented a substantive contribution to the development of TCDC, especially within and by the United Nations development system.

11. The Kuwait Declaration on Technical Co-operation among Developing Countries of 5 June 1977, following four regional intergovernmental meetings on the subject, states that "TCDC is a historical imperative brought about by the need for a new international order. It is a conscious, systematic and politically motivated process developed to create a framework of multiple links between developing countries."[7] The Kuwait Declaration was recognized in resolution CM/RES.560 (XXIX), adopted by the Council of Ministers of the Organization of African Unity at its twenty-ninth ordinary session, held at Libreville from 23 June to 5 July 1977. It was further endorsed by the Assembly of Heads of State and Government of the Organization of African Unity at its fourteenth ordinary session, held at Libreville from 23 June to 5 July 1977,[8] and by the Council of Ministers of the Organization of African Unity at its thirty-first ordinary session, held at Khartoum from 7 to 8 July 1978.

12. Technical co-operation among developing countries has emerged as a new dimension of international co-operation for development, which gives expression to the developing world's determination to achieve national and collective self-reliance and to the need to bring about the new international economic order. Its emergence and rationale should therefore be viewed in this global perspective in the light of experience gained from international technical assistance and in the light of the conclusions reached by previous United Nations world conferences that had a bearing on development and co-operation.

13. TCDC as well as other forms of co-operation among all countries must be based on strict observance of national sovereignty, economic independence, equal rights and non-interference in domestic affairs of nations, irrespective of their size, level of development and social and economic systems.

14. The strengthening of TCDC must constitute an important component of any future strategy which seeks to accelerate development, to enhance human dignity and progress, and to improve the performance of the world economy as a whole.

II. OBJECTIVES

15. The basic objectives of TCDC, which are interdependent and mutually supportive, contribute to the wider objectives of the development of the developing countries and international development co-operation. They reinforce those of closely related forms of co-operation, including economic co-operation among developing countries, for which TCDC is a key instrument. The objectives are:

---

[4]See A/CONF.79/12.
[5]See A/33/206, annexes I and II.
[6]DP/69.
[7]See A/CONF.79/PC/18.
[8]See A/32/310, annex I.

(a) To foster the self-reliance of developing countries through the enhancement of their creative capacity to find solutions to their development problems in keeping with their own aspirations, values and special needs;

(b) To promote and strengthen collective self-reliance among developing countries through exchanges of experience, the pooling, sharing and utilization of their technical resources, and the development of their complementary capacities;

(c) To strengthen the capacity of developing countries to identify and analyze together the main issues of their development and to formulate the requisite strategies in the conduct of their international economic relations, through pooling of knowledge available in those countries through joint studies by their existing institutions, with a view to establishing the new international economic order;

(d) To increase the quantum and enhance the quality of international co-operation as well as to improve the effectiveness of the resources devoted to over-all technical co-operation through the pooling of capacities;

(e) To strengthen existing technological capacities in the developing countries, including the traditional sector, to improve the effectiveness with which such capacities are used and to create new capacities and capabilities and in this context to promote the transfer of technology and skills appropriate to their resource endowments and the development potential of the developing countries so as to strengthen their individual and collective self-reliance;

(f) To increase and improve communications among developing countries, leading to a greater awareness of common problems and wider access to available knowledge and experience as well as the creation of new knowledge in tackling problems of development;

(g) To improve the capacity of developing countries for the absorption and adaptation of technology and skill to meet their specific developmental needs;

(h) To recognize and respond to the problems and requirements of the least developed, landlocked, island developing and most seriously affected countries;

(i) To enable developing countries to attain a greater degree of participation in international economic activities and to expand international co-operation.

16. TCDC clearly serves many other purposes, such as overcoming attitudinal barriers, increasing developing countries' confidence in each other's technical capabilities and enhancing the process of harmonization of their interests so as to take fully into account, within the context of the fundamental concept of solidarity, their specific subregional, regional, and interregional characterisics, particularly by identifying priorities in such fields as transport and communications, employment, development and exchange of human resources, as well as agriculture and industry.

III. ACTION TO BE TAKEN

17. The recommendations formulated below should strengthen and support co-operation among developing countries, for example, and without implying an indication of priority, through the implementation of current activities and programmes of action decided upon by the developing countries, in such fields as employment and development of human resources, fisheries, food and agriculture, health, industrialization, information, integration of women in development, monetary and financial co-operation, raw materials, science and technology, technical co-operation and consultancy service, telecommunications, tourism, trade, and transport and communications. These recommendations should also facilitate the formulation of programmes of co-operation in other sectors.

A. Action at the national level

18. The primary objectives of the following recommendations for action at the national level are: to increase the awareness in each developing country of its own capabilities, skills and experience, and of those available in other developing countries; to establish and strengthen the necessary supportive arrangements—institutions, information, human and other resources—on which TCDC must be firmly based; to identify specific opportunities for TCDC, and to enhance the capacities of developing countries to organize and implement expeditiously and effectively projects with a TCDC dimension. While such actions would clearly be the responsibility of each developing country, the support of other developing countries, developed countries and international organizations, where requested, could make important contributions. In the implementation of the recommendations set out below, the United Nations development system would be expected to extend its fullest support when requested to do so by Governments.

19. Bilateral co-operation among developing countries represents an important form of TCDC and an instrument for forging links between national and collective self-reliance. Therefore, the main aim of recommendations concerning bilateral co-operation is to stimulate, intensify and improve it in substance, form and mechanisms.

Recommendation 1. *National programming for technical co-operation among developing countries*

20. In formulating its national development plan or programme, each developing country should endeavour to identify its potential for TCDC. Such a process should include evaluation of its experience in relevant sectors of economic and social development that may have a bearing on the needs of other developing countries. On this basis, the Government may consider national requirements in research, technology, skills, consultancy services and training facilities and employment strategies that can be met most effectively through co-operation with other developing countries, as well as the contributions in respect of these which it can make for the benefit of other developing countries.

Recommendation 2. *Adoption of policies and regulations favourable to technical co-operation among developing countries*

21. Each developing country should consider adopting policies favourable to TCDC, and working out the legal and administrative framework for effective and equitable co-operation, taking into account practices already established on the basis of formal conventions, thus ensuring their widest possible applicability and acceptance. The framework should cover the administrative and legal arrangements concerning the entry, employment, obligations, privileges and immunities of experts and consultants, arrangements concerning fellowships, the use of contractors and other specialist services, entry of equipment and supplies, fiscal and currency regimes favourable to TCDC and also financial arrangements aimed at an equitable sharing of costs. It should also cover appropriate administrative and legal arrangements embracing, *inter alia*, arrangements to facilitate the sending of technical and professional personnel abroad without jeopardizing the terms and prospects of their regular employment on their return, as well as the provision of consultancy services, the supply of equipment and the granting of fellowships and apprenticeships.

Recommendation 3. *National mechanisms for promoting technical co-operation among developing countries*

22. Each developing country should, as appropriate, organize flexible mechanisms or strengthen them where they already exist in order to promote TCDC, to facilitate the co-ordination of

TCDC activities at the national level and their incorporation into the national development programmes. Such mechanisms may involve the participation of public and private sector representatives to enable close interaction with government bodies and other sectoral organizations.

Recommendation 4. *The strengthening of national information systems for technical co-operation among developing countries*

23. Each developing country should take adequate steps to strengthen the gathering, processing and dissemination of information covering the availability of national capacities, knowledge and experience for application and use in TCDC, if necessary with the support of the information systems of the United Nations development system, and particularly of the Information Referral System (INRES) of the United Nations Development Programme (UNDP), as well as official, professional and other sources. Governments of developing countries should further intensify their co-operation with the appropriate bodies at the regional, interregional and global levels for the pooling of such information so as to facilitate the communication to other developing countries of the availability of such resources and opportunities for TCDC. These bodies should secure the information for TCDC from Governments and entities officially designated by them and disseminate it through the channels established for this purpose by Governments.

Recommendation 5. *The improvement of existing institutions*

24. Since a strong institutional base is essential for viable TCDC, developing countries should individually identify and assess the effectiveness and potential of national institutions for the purpose, and adopt measures, wherever necessary, to improve their effectiveness and enhance their potentials. National organizations of developing countries working on common problems can make valuable contributions to the expansion of TCDC. Such organizations could organize operational collaboration so as to achieve a mutuality of relationships. Such collaboration would strengthen their own capabilities by sharing work and experience with others working on the same problems at various levels of complexity and in diverse environments, and also, where feasible, by sharing responsibilities for common training activities.

Recommendation 6. *Promotion of national research and training centres with multinational scope*

25. Developing countries should encourage existing national research and training centres to broaden their scope of activities to include programmes and projects which are of interest to several countries at a subregional, regional and interregional level. While existing national centres should be utilized for this purpose to the maximum extent possible, where necessary, new centres may be created for the same purpose.

Recommendation 7. *The promotion of greater technological self-reliance*

26. Developing countries should make every effort to strengthen their scientific and technological capabilities to suit their special needs, values and resource endowments by formulating, where necessary, technology plans as an integral part of their national development plans; establishing scientific and technological data banks; encouraging indigenous research and development activities for the attainment of their development objectives; combining research efforts and sharing their results with one another by means of agreements on scientific and technical co-operation; strengthening national design, national laboratories, research centres and scientific and other institutions; and linking their national research and development institutions, where appropriate, to those in other developing countries, including linkage

through the regional centres on transfer and development of technology. Developing countries should undertake special efforts to strengthen their national potentials in engineering and consultancy services by improving the professional standards, organizing training and research. Broad exchange of experiences in this field among developing countries is an indispensable component of national and collective self-reliance.

Recommendation 8. *The formulation, orientation and sharing of policy experiences with respect to science and technology*

27. In view of the important role of science and technology in the development of developing countries, and bearing in mind the successful experience of several developing countries in applying science and technology in their development process, developing countries should, wherever possible, exchange among themselves their experiences in the formulation and implementation of their plans and policies for the orientation of science and the transfer and development of technology to their own development objectives, needs and capabilities.

Recommendation 9. *The promotion of greater self-reliance in the economic and social spheres*

28. The Governments of developing countries should intensify their efforts to promote national and collective self-reliance by strengthening their mutual contracts and communications, by exchanging experience, and by undertaking programmes and projects, including joint ones, in areas of mutual interest in the economic and social sectors.

Recommendation 10. *Technical co-operation among developing countries in the cultural spheres*

29. The Governments of developing countries should, in order to affirm the cultural identity of their peoples and to enrich and strengthen their collective capacity with a greater awareness of the culture and heritage of other developing countries, increasingly employ TCDC mechanisms to foster cultural and educational links and to strengthen mutual knowledge by promoting exchanges and co-operation in the social sciences, education and culture.

Recommendation 11. *The encouragement of technical co-operation among developing countries through professional and technical organizations*

30. The Governments of developing countries should encourage and facilitate co-operation among professional and technical organizations in their TCDC activities in their own countries and in other developing countries.

Recommendation 12. *The expansion of TCDC through national public and private enterprises and institutions*

31. Having regard to the important and growing contribution that enterprises and institutions in the public sector are making to national development in the developing countries and the rich fund of experience acquired by them over the years, the Governments of developing countries should endeavour to establish or strengthen suitable arrangements to encourage and maintain co-operation and communication between public enterprises and institutions in their own countries and those in other developing countries, especially with a view to promoting closer technical collaboration. Similarly, Governments of developing countries should aim at encouraging comparable arrangements with regard to national private enterprises and institutions, where applicable.

Recommendation 13. *Information and education programmes in support of technical co-operation among developing countries*

32. Governments and non-governmental organizations of developing countries should undertake long-term information and education programmes to strengthen their own cultural identities, to encourage greater awareness of their common development problems and opportunities, to mobilize public support for self-reliance, and to break down attitudinal barriers to the expansion of TCDC. The United Nations system should lend intensive support to such programmes, seeking special additional resources for that purpose.

Recommendation 14. *The expansion of bilateral technical links*

33. In order to facilitate sustained and widening technical co-operation among developing countries, and since bilateral arrangements constitute one of the fundamental aspects of this co-operation, the Governments of developing countries should endeavour to expand bilateral arrangements for promoting TCDC through such mechanisms as co-operative agreements and programmes, joint commissions, the regular exchange of information and experience, and the support of initiatives in the public and private sectors. In this respect developing countries should undertake special efforts to intensify TCDC through long-term programmes and projects by enhancing the programming and undertaking special measures for the successful implementation of those programmes and also by establishing direct linkages among similar institutions.

B. Action at the subregional and regional levels

34. TCDC should be conducted by each State, and at the subregional and regional levels jointly by all concerned. The following recommendations for action at the subregional and regional levels should take into account, *inter alia,* the need to:

(a) Strengthen existing subregional and regional institutions and organizations and thus their capacity to serve better the needs of each Government concerned in its efforts to co-operate with others;

(b) Develop and strengthen interinstitutional links in important, high-priority substantive areas, such as those identified at the regional preparatory intergovernmental meetings for the Conference, designed to draw on the capabilities and experiences available in the region;

(c) Reinforce the capacities available for data collection and analysis in order to provide systematic and updated information for decision makers at the national subregional and regional levels; and

(d) Improve regional information systems for TCDC, particularly those related to technical co-operation needs which cannot always be expressed simply in the traditional terms of skills, equipment and training requirements.

Recommendation 15. *The strengthening of subregional and regional institutions and organizations*

35. All Governments should endeavour to strengthen the capacities of subregional and regional organizations to implement TCDC activities and projects. In this connexion the United Nations development system should support those endeavours, particularly through the regional commissions, in close collaboration with the regional bureaux of UNDP and with other bodies of the United Nations development system which have regional structures or divisions.

Recommendation 16. *The identification, development and implementation of initiatives for technical co-operation among developing countries*

36. The appropriate subregional and regional intergovernmental organizations, at the request of and in close collaboration with the countries concerned and with the support of the United Nations regional commissions and other United Nations organizations, should undertake analyses of technical co-operation needs and capacities within the respective subregion or region to assist Governments of developing countries in the identification, development and implementation of TCDC initiatives in agreed priority areas.

Recommendation 17. *The enhancement of contributions by professional and technical organizations*

37. The appropriate subregional and regional intergovernmental organizations, at the request of and in close collaboration with the countries concerned, and with the support of the United Nations regional commissions and other United Nations organizations, should conduct appropriate studies at the request of the Governments concerned and recommend to Governments action programmes to enhance the contributions of the professional and technical organizations concerned in support of TCDC.

Recommendation 18. *The creation of new links for technical co-operation among developing countries in important substantive areas*

38. The appropriate subregional and regional intergovernmental organizations, including or with the support of the regional commissions, at the request of and in close consultation with the countries involved, should formulate and support TCDC activities and projects at the subregional and regional levels in such areas of particular concern as may be identified by Governments individually or jointly. These TCDC activities and projects should facilitate and strengthen linkages among the national organizations working to resolve developmental problems, and those concerned with research and development and the adaptation of technology.

Recommendation 19. *Promotion of complementary industrial and agricultural projects at the subregional and regional levels*

39. The appropriate subregional and regional intergovernmental organizations, in view of the potential for complementarities, should promote joint projects in industry and agriculture where the parties concerned specialize in their respective areas of complementarity, the products of which would have preferential access to the market of the parties concerned in the subregion or region.

Recommendation 20. *The improvement of regional information for technical co-operation among developing countries*

40. The appropriate subregional and regional intergovernmental organizations, including, or with the support of, the United Nations regional commissions, at the request of and in close collaboration with the countries concerned and with the support of other United Nations organizations should:

(a) Contribute towards improving both the qualitative and quantitative aspects of the Information Referral System (INRES) and similar systems being developed by other components of the United Nations development system in specialized technical fields in widening their coverage and utilization of information on technical co-operation among developing countries;

(b) Ensure the effective, speedy and economical pooling and dissemination of information on the technical co-operation requirements and capacities of the developing countries within each region drawing on, *inter alia,* various potential mechanisms such as institutional networks and professional journals, which should also aim at overcoming language barriers;

(c) Prepare or harmonize, where necessary, subregional and regional standards in TCDC information flow.

Recommendation 21. *Support to national research and training centres with multinational scope*

41. The appropriate subregional and regional intergovernmental organizations, with the support of the United Nations development system, should provide, at the request of interested developing countries, the necessary support to enable national research and training centres with multinational scope to operate effectively in order to promote TCDC.

C. Action at the interregional level

42. A prime objective of TCDC is to enable the developing countries to benefit from the widest access to accumulated experience in efforts to deal with comparable development problems. It is now recognized that, for a variety of reasons, the experience and knowledge needed by a developing country in a given region may well be found, if not within the region, then in another region. Moreover, as countries in a given region may have adopted similar approaches to problems, new approaches may be found by drawing upon and distilling experience from outside the region. Interregional co-operation offers considerable potential advantages and constitutes a substantial and important opportunity for TCDC.

43. A wide variety of interregional intergovernmental organizations of developing countries exists. Some such organizations are of a political character, others pursue common social and economic goals, and yet others function in specific technical or economic fields. These organizations, institutions or arrangements should be fully mobilized to promote, support or conduct TCDC projects and programmes, within their respective terms of reference.

Recommendation 22. *The development and strengthening of interregional co-operation*

44. Governments of developing countries that are members of interregional organizations, institutions or arrangements should, as appropriate, through such interregional organizations, institutions or arrangements, and in collaboration with their subregional and regional intergovernmental organizations and, as appropriate, with the assistance of organizations of the United Nations development system, in particular the regional commissions, consider initiating *inter alia*:

(a) An evaluation of the function of TCDC in their common organizations, institutions or arrangements, and their capacity to promote TCDC further;

(b) The necessary measures to strengthen the interregional linkages between subregional and regional organizations with similar interests and complementary capacities;

(c) The joint identification of development problems that are interregional in scope and have a TCDC dimension; and

(d) Joint programmes to be undertaken by appropriate interregional organizations or at an interregional level by any two or more entities belonging to different regions, and the identification of additional needs or organizational gaps where new arrangements may be called for.

D. Action at the global level

45. The entire United Nations development system must be permeated by the spirit of TCDC and all its organizations should play a prominent role as promoters and catalysts of TCDC. The United Nations Development Programme, the specialized agencies and other bodies of the United Nations family, including the regional commissions, have already directed a number of their activities towards TCDC. The decisions and recommendations of the United Nations Conference on Technical Co-operation among Developing Countries should lead to the strengthening and expansion of these efforts in order to complement further those made at the national, subregional, regional and interregional levels.

Recommendation 23. *The enhancement of national and collective self-reliance*

46. In view of the fact that the achievement of national and collective self-reliance through the release and development of indigenous capacities necessitates an important change in emphasis, the thrust of international technical co-operation should be increasingly directed towards enhancing the capacities of developing countries to help themselves and each other. The use of the resources of the United Nations Development Programme and other multilateral and bilateral agencies should reflect this change in emphasis.

Recommendation 24. *The exchange of development experience*

47. Since a great deal of benefit is to be derived by developing countries from sharing each other's experiences, the organizations of the United Nations development system should, at the request of interested developing countries, provide assistance in their respective sectors in preparing programmes and projects through which the rich experience accumulated in these countries in dealing with the problems connected with improving the living conditions of their populations could be shared and extensively applied.

Recommendation 25. *The fostering of global technical collaboration*

48. Governments and international development assistance organizations, in seeking to expand the potential and outreach of TCDC, should foster collaborative associations among national and international technical organizations that are working in the same development problem area so as to give support to TCDC projects agreed upon by developing countries, at the request of countries concerned. Expansion of such problem-solving networks should be in accordance with the objectives identified by the developing countries concerned in their TCDC projects.

Recommendation 26. *The improvement of information flows*

49. To encourage and intensify the collection, processing, analysis and dissemination at the global level of information on the capacities and needs of developing countries, the Information Referral System (INRES) and other related information systems should be further improved, developed and expanded. They should comprehensively cover the needs that might be met through TCDC in dealing with specific, detailed development problems. The Inquiry Service of INRES should be expanded at an early date in order to be able to match speedily the specific needs of developing countries with available capacities in order to improve channels for the wider use of experts, consultants, training facilities, equipment and other capacities of developing countries through bilateral or multilateral TCDC arrangements. For improved efficiency and better service to developing countries, appropriate linkages should be established between INRES and the information systems of other organizations of the United Nations development system and of the subregional and regional intergovernmental organizations.

50. In order to improve further the efficiency of INRES and to develop it appropriately, the Administrator of the United Nations Development Programme should initiate an evaluation and assessment of the functioning of the System.

Recommendation 27. *Control of the "brain drain" from developing countries*

51. In view of the global nature of the problem of the migration of professional and skilled manpower from developing countries and of such manpower's potential as an asset for TCDC, the organizations of the United Nations development system and the specialized international agencies which deal with migration should assist the developing countries, at their request, to formulate measures for strengthening their capacities to encourage patterns of voluntary migration in the interests of their development, including not only selective migration of skilled people between developing countries, but also the return of scientific, professional and technical personnel living outside their countries of origin, taking into account work already initiated on a bilateral and multilateral basis as well as relevant resolutions adopted in various United Nations forums.

Recommendation 28. *Measures in favour of economically or geographically disadvantaged developing countries*

52. Effective practical measures should be taken by Governments and multilateral technical co-operation agencies for dealing with the special problems and requirements of the least developed, landlocked, island and most seriously affected countries in order to increase their capacities to contribute to and benefit from TCDC activities. In accordance with the decisions embodied in the resolutions of the General Assembly and other bodies concerned, a special effort should be made by developing countries as a whole, with the support of developed countries and of the United Nations development system, to channel through TCDC the technical and financial resources to assist them.

Rcommendation 29. *Measures in favour of newly independent countries*

53. Special efforts should be made by all countries as well as the United Nations development system to support TCDC activities and projects in the newly independent countries.

Recommendation 30. *The strengthening of transport and communications among developing countries*

54. Bearing in mind the fact that the strengthening of transport and communications among developing countries is a necessary condition if TCDC is to become a major element in the development process, the Governments of developing countries should, on the basis of studies carried out by themselves, and by the organizations of the United Nations system when so requested, make specific and sustained efforts to strengthen, improve and maintain all means of transport and communications between their countries. In this context, all countries, the United Nations system and other international organizations should effectively support the implementation of programmes of the Transport and Communications Decade in Africa.

Recommendation 31. *Maximization of the use of developing countries' capacities*

55. In designing, formulating and executing technical co-operation projects, Governments and, at the request of developing countries, intergovernmental and other organizations concerned with supporting international development efforts should make the greatest possible use of local capabilities, including local expertise and consultancy firms. Where institutions and expertise of the requisite level, quality and relevance are not available locally, developing countries should have the option of obtaining such technical resources from other developing

countries, taking due account of factors of quality, cost, delivery schedules and other related conditions. Similarly, the placement of fellowships and the procurement of equipment should also be directed towards other developing countries, wherever their facilities and experience are suitable.

Recommendation 32. *Activities for technical co-operation among developing countries by the organizations of the United Nations development system in their respective fields*

56. The governing bodies of the organizations of the United Nations development system should make every effort to mobilize their organizations in order to contribute to implementing this Plan of Action on a continuing and intensive basis, both in their respective fields of competence and in multidisciplinary joint action. Such efforts should focus on promotional, co-ordinating, operational, and financial issues and should, *inter alia,* be aimed at:

(a) Identifying TCDC solutions, or TCDC contributions to solutions, for specific development problems, *inter alia,* by incorporating TCDC aspects into international meetings and/or organizing when necessary international meetings on specific fields of interest to developing countries with relevance to TCDC;

(b) Applying TCDC approaches and techniques in their programmes;

(c) Supporting on request the preparation and execution of TCDC projects;

(d) Developing new ideas and approaches for realizing the full potential of TCDC and, for this purpose, undertake the necessary studies and analyses;

(e) Developing, strengthening or reorienting specific sectoral or subregional and regional information systems, and establishing functional linkages between such systems and INRES with a view to their effective utilization;

(f) Organizing and assisting public information support for TCDC in their respective areas of competence;

(g) Monitoring and reviewing the implementation of their TCDC activities;

(h) Utilizing to the maximum extent possible the inputs available locally and those from other developing countries in keeping with paragraph 55.

Recommendation 33. *Internal arrangements for technical co-operation among developing countries in the organizations of the United Nations development system*

57. In order to pursue vigorously TCDC policies and measures at all levels in different sectors of development, all organizations and bodies of the United Nations development system should, if they have not already done so, reorient their internal policies and procedures in order to respond adequately to the principles and objectives of TCDC. These organizations should also make the necessary internal adjustments and arrangements in their secretariats in order to integrate TCDC in their programmes of work. These arrangements should be result-oriented and should promote TCDC in the operational activities of these organizations.

Recommendation 34. *Strengthening the capacity of the UNDP for the promotion and support of TCDC*

58. In view of the wide implications and the importance of TCDC and the number of tasks which need to be carried out at the global level, and bearing in mind the importance that TCDC must assume in UNDP as an integral part of its activities, the Administrator of UNDP should

take further steps to give the necessary orientation to the activities, programmes and projects of UNDP in order to support the objectives of TCDC. These steps should include the strengthening of the capacity of the UNDP administration to work in close collaboration with the regional commissions and with regional offices of other organs and agencies of the United Nations development system through their respective headquarters, and also to respond more effectively in initiatives from subregional, regional and interregional intergovernmental organizations and groupings.

59. In this context and bearing in mind its existing function,[9] the Special Unit, which should continue to be financed from the administrative budget of UNDP, should be strengthened in order to assist the Administrator of UNDP to carry out the functions described below:

(a) Assisting Governments at their request and, where appropriate, in full collaboration with the relevant organs, organizations and bodies of the United Nations development system, to undertake TCDC programmes and activities in order to achieve the objectives of TCDC;

(b) Developing, in full collaboration with the participating and executing agencies and regional commissions, new ideas, concepts and approaches for promoting technical co-operation among developing countries, and for this purpose, arranging for the necessary studies and analyses to be undertaken and submitted to the Governments for consideration and approval in the intergovernmental body mentioned in paragraph 62;

(c) Co-ordinating the activities of the UNDP in the field of TCDC with those of the participating and executing agencies as well as the regional commissions in the field of TCDC;

(d) Expanding, strengthening and promoting the efficient use of INRES and establishing appropriate linkages with national and regional information systems and/or focal points;

(e) Promoting channels of communication with appropriate intergovernmental and non-governmental organizations so as to widen the awareness of TCDC and thereby generating financial and other support for TCDC activities;

(f) Servicing the intergovernmental arrangement referred to in paragraph 62;

(g) Preparing modifications in the policies, rules and procedures of UNDP, in accordance with relevant decisions of the General Assembly and the UNDP Governing Council, with a view to improving the Programme's capacity to implement TCDC and assisting, at their request, other organs and organizations of the United Nations system in this regard;

(h) In full collaboration with the organs, organizations and bodies concerned of the United Nations system, preparing progress reports on the implementation of the Plan of Action and making suggestions to expedite progress through new actions and initiatives for the consideration of the intergovernmental body referred to in paragraph 62.

Recommendation 35. *Support by developed countries for technical co-operation among developing countries*

60. Developed countries and their institutions should give their full support to TCDC initiatives by *inter alia:*

(a) Increasing their voluntary contributions to the operational programmes of the United Nations development system in order to permit a greater quantum of multilateral technical co-operation funds to be devoted to supporting TCDC;

(b) Providing financial support on a voluntary basis to technical co-operation between two or more developing countries and to institutions in developing countries that have a TCDC outreach potential;

---

[9] Annex to DP/69.

(c) Accelerating the process of untying their aid resources, so as to make possible more rapid progress in the promotion and strengthening of TCDC;

(d) Giving, in their economic and technical co-operation activities, due priority to intercountry projects and programmes at the bilateral, subregional, regional and interregional levels which promote TCDC;

(e) Making qualitative improvements, if they have not yet done so, in their policies and procedures related to technical co-operation, in order to be able to support TCDC activities and projects at the request of participating developing countries so as to contribute to the greater reliance by those countries on resources available locally or in other developing countries.

Recommendation 36. *The harmonization of development assistance with technical co-operation among developing countries*

61. TCDC activities and traditional technical co-operation and development assistance to which the developed countries contribute should be productively linked. Developed countries should take fully into account, on a continuing basis, the goals established for TCDC activities when formulating their development assistance and technical co-operation policies. Developed countries, if they have not yet done so, should also institute changes in their procedures for furnishing technical and capital assistance to foster TCDC and a greater measure of national and collective self-reliance among developing countries.

Recommendation 37. *Intergovernmental arrangements*

62. Recognizing that the UNDP, as the principal funding source of technical co-operation within the United Nations development system, has particular responsibility for the promotion and support of TCDC, in close collaboration with the specialized agencies, programmes and organizations of the United Nations development system, the over-all intergovernmental review of TCDC within the United Nations system should be entrusted by the General Assembly to a high-level meeting of representatives of all States participating in the United Nations Development Programme. This meeting should be convened by the Administrator of the United Nations Development Programme and should, after annual meetings in 1980 and 1981, be held biennially. These meetings should be held in the same place as, and prior to, sessions of the UNDP Governing Council and should carry out the following functions:

(a) Reviewing the progress made in implementing the tasks entrusted to the United Nations development system by the Buenos Aires Plan of Action;

(b) Ensuring that efforts to strengthen TCDC are sustained within the United Nations development system;

(c) Supporting new policies and innovative approaches to further the development of TCDC;

(d) Considering the availability of financial resources and their effective use by the United Nations development system, without prejudice to existing programmes;

(e) Ensuring co-ordination of the promotional and operational TCDC activities of the United Nations development system.

63. United Nations organs, organizations and bodies, including the regional commissions, and other subregional, regional and interregional intergovernmental organizations should participate actively in the work of these meetings.

64. These meetings shall report to the General Assembly through the UNDP Governing Council and the Economic and Social Council.

Recommendation 38. *Financial arrangements for technical co-operation among developing countries*

65. In view of the fact that the financing of TCDC activities is primarily the responsibility of developing countries themselves, it will nevertheless be necessary for the developed countries and the United Nations development system to support these activities financially without prejudice to the decision-making control by the developing countries of these TCDC activities. Financial participation in and support for TCDC projects and activities should include, *inter alia,* the following:

(a) Developing countries should determine norms and mechanisms appropriate to them in the context of their participation in the financing of TCDC activities at the national, bilateral, subregional, regional and interregional levels, with due consideration for the constraints faced by the least developed, landlocked, island developing and most seriously affected developing countries and newly independent countries;

(b) Regional and international funds, development banks and other intergovernmental financial institutions and aid agencies should, within their respective terms of reference, make special efforts to finance TCDC projects and activities, and, as appropriate, make adjustments in their policies and procedures, to promote TCDC;

(c) Developing countries which may wish to do so should consider earmarking a percentage of their Indicative Planning Figure of UNDP at the national level, for financing TCDC projects at the bilateral and subregional levels;

(d) Regional Indicative Planning Figures of UNDP should be used to the maximum possible extent on the basis of regional priorities, for financing TCDC projects and activities. The responsibility for identifying and initiating such projects and activities should lie with the developing countries of the region concerned;

(e) A sizeable proportion of interregional and global Indicative Planning Figures of UNDP should be devoted to the financing of TCDC projects and activities requested by two or more developing countries of different regions. The management of these resources should be conducted in close consultation with the developing countries concerned;

(f) The United Nations development system should explore additional sources of finance for TCDC projects and activities including those of an interregional and global nature;

(g) Flows of development assistance should be increased on a predictable, assured and continuous basis;

(h) Developed countries should provide on a voluntary basis and without prejudice to existing programmes, additional financial support for TCDC projects and activities, for example through third-country financing arrangements, through increased contributions to different national, subregional, regional, interregional or international organizations, including UNDP;

(i) All organizations of the United Nations development system should allocate an increasing proportion of their resources for TCDC activities and projects;

(j) In this context, special efforts should be made by the United Nations development system, other aid-giving agencies, developed and developing countries, to strengthen the capacity of the least developed, landlocked, island developing, most seriously affected and newly independent countries, to participate effectively in TCDC activities and projects.

Notes

Introduction
[1] United Nations General Assembly Resolution 31/179, December 21, 1976.

[2] Lynn White, *Medieval Technology and Social Change* (Oxford: Oxford University Press, 1966), p. 38.

Chapter 1
[1] "The Determinants and Consequences of Population Trends" (United Nations, 1973), p. 10, in Nougier: *Géographie humaine préhistorique,* 1959, pp. 14–15.

[2] Concise Report on the World Population Situation. United Nations. 1978, p. 1.

Chapter 2
[1] *Encyclopaedia Britannica.* "History of the Indian Subcontinent," XV Edition, Macropaedia, 1974, Volume 9, p. 411.

[2] Nikhil Sur, "The Bahar Famine of 1770," *The Indian Economic and Social History Review,* Volume XIII, 1976. No. 4, p. 531.

[3] W.W. Rostow, *The Stages of Economic Growth* (Cambridge: Cambridge University Press, 1960).

[4] Dennis A. Rondinelli, *International Organization,* Vol. 30, No. 4. Autumn 1976, p. 573. Mr. Rondinelli was Director of the Graduate Planning Program at New York's Syracuse University when he wrote the paper.

[5] Yusuf J. Ahmad, "Project Identification, Analysis and Preparation in Developing Countries," *Development and Change,* July 1975, p. 85.

Chapter 3
[1] Armand Van Dormael, *Bretton Woods* (New York: Holmes and Meier, 1978).

[2] "The Kennedy Round Estimated Effects on Trade Barriers," UNCTAD, 1968.

[3]Its membership is as follows: Australia, Austria, Belgium, Canada, Denmark, Eire, Finland, France, Germany, Greece, Iceland, Italy, Japan, Luxembourg, Netherlands, New Zealand, Norway, Portugal, Spain, Sweden, Switzerland, Turkey, United Kingdom, United States.

[4]Amon J. Nsekela, Address at the University of Manchester, November 20, 1976.

[5]The membership of the CMEA includes: Bulgaria, Cuba, Czechoslovakia, Hungary, Mongolia, Poland, Romania, USSR, and Vietnam.

[6]Ye T. Usenko, ed., *The Multilateral Economic Co-operation of Socialist States* (Moscow: Progress Publishers, 1977), p. 11.

Chapter 4   [1]Donald E. Lach, *Asia in the Making of Europe* Vol. I. Book 2 (University of Chicago Press, 1965), p. 513.

[2]Harry Magdoff, *The Age of Imperialism* (New York: Monthly Review Press, 1969), p. 69.

[3]Daniel Bell, ed. *Toward the Year 2000: Work In Progress* (Boston: Beacon Press, 1967), p. 315.

[4]*Multinational Corporations in World Development* (United Nations, 1973), p. 6.

[5]Richard J. Barnet and Ronald J. Müller, *Global Reach: The Power of Multinational Corporations* (New York: Simon and Schuster, 1974), p. 147.

[6]"Nestlé Kills Babies," Swiss Action Groups for Development Policy, 1974, Geneva; "The Baby Killer," "War on Want," London, 1974.

[7]*Transnational Corporations in World Development: A Re-examination* (United Nations, 1978), p. 6.

[8]Ibid., p. 46.

[9]Irving Komanoff, "Long and Short," *Barrons*, January 17, 1977—A panel discussion in which Irving Komanoff of Herzfield and Stern asked the question; Charles T. Maxwell, Senior Vice-President of Cyrus J. Lawrence answered.

Chapter 5   [1]*Asian-African Conference, Bandung* (Information Service of Indonesia, 1955), p. 27.

[2]Thomas P. Ronan, "London Disputes Peiping on Crash," *New York Times*, April 18, 1955, p. 1.

[3]Mohammed El Farra, *Nationalism in the United States*, 1964.

[4]Mohammed Ahmed El Khawas, *Voting Patterns of the Afro-Asian Group* (Ann Arbor: University Microfilms).

[5]United Nations General Assembly Resolution 1995 (XIX), December 30, 1964.

Chapter 6

[1]David Housego, *Times* (London), January 25, 1971.

[2]*1971 OPEC Annual Review and Record* (OPEC, Vienna, 1972).

[3]Leon Howell and Michael Morrow, *Asia, Oil Politics and the Energy Crisis* (IDOC North-America, 1974), p. 30.

[4]In 1970 the price had been under $2 per average barrel of Persian Gulf crude oil.

Chapter 7

[1]*Salient Features of Economic Co-operation Among Developing Countries* (United Nations, 1977), p. 10.

[2]Brazil, Chile, Egypt, Greece, India, Israel, Mexico, Pakistan, Peru, Philippines, Republic of Korea, Spain, Tunisia, Turkey, Uruguay, Yugoslavia.

[3]UNCTAD, *Cooperative Exchange of Skills Among Developing Countries*, p. VI, February 8, 1978.

Chapter 9

[1]E. Oteiza, A. Rahman, R. Green, and C. Vaitsos, *TCDC As a New Dimension of International Co-operation for Development* (United Nations, 1978).

[2]Muchkund Dubey, *Institutional Arrangements at the International Level to Promote and Conduct TCDC* (United Nations, 1978).

[3]J.G. Odero-Jowi, *Rules, Regulations, Procedures and Practices of the U.N. Development System in Recruiting Experts, Subcontracting, Procuring Equipment and Providing Fellowships* (UNDP, 1978).

Chapter 10

[1]A workshop on TCDC organized by UNDP. It was attended by representatives from 34 professional and technical associations, including intergovernmental, nongovernmental and media organizations. The workshop met during the conference and addressed itself to five main questions: 1) Science and technology policies: in whose interests? 2) Researchers, consultants and professionals: what is their contribution? 3) Human dimensions in TCDC—where are they? 4) Attitudinal and communications barriers—how to overcome them? 5) Options in rural development: How, what, where to select?

[2]Robert Jackson, *A Study of the Capactiy of the U.N. Development System*. Vol. II. (United Nations, 1968), pp. 5–6.

[3]Michael Geoghegan, *Third World and Global Society* (New World Forum, 1976), p. 33.

[4]IPFs show the allocations from the UNDP budget during a program period.

Index

About the Author

B.P. MENON is a journalist working for the United Nations in New York. His articles on travel and international affairs have been published in newspapers and magazines in many countries. He is the author of "Global Dialogue" (1977) and "World Orders—A Comic Book" (1978).